GROWING UP IN GOD'S FAMILY

BIBLE STUDY GUIDE

From the Bible-teaching ministry of

Charles R. Swindoll

INSIGHT FOR LIVING

Charles R. Swindoll graduated in 1963 from Dallas Theological Seminary and has served in pastorates over thirty years, including more than twenty-two years at the First Evangelical Free Church of Fullerton, California. His sermon messages have been aired over radio since 1979 as the "Insight for Living" broadcast. In addition to his church and radio ministries, Chuck enjoys writing. As a best-selling author, he has written numerous books and booklets on a variety of subjects.

Based on the outlines and transcripts of Chuck's sermons, the study guide text is co-authored by Bryce Klabunde, a graduate of Biola University and Dallas Theological Seminary. He also wrote the Living Insights sections.

Editor in Chief:
Cynthia Swindoll

Coauthor of Text:
Bryce Klabunde

Assistant Editor:
Wendy Peterson

Copy Editors:
Deborah Gibbs
Cheryl Gilmore
Glenda Schlahta

Designer:
Gary Lett

Publishing System Specialist:
Bob Haskins

Director, Communications Division:
Deedee Snyder

Manager, Creative Services:
Alene Cooper

Project Supervisor:
Kim Winburn

Print Production Manager:
John Norton

Printer:
Sinclair Printing Company

Unless otherwise identified, all Scripture references are from the New American Standard Bible, © The Lockman Foundation 1960, 1962, 1963, 1968, 1971, 1972, 1973, 1975, 1977. Used by permission.

Scripture taken from the Holy Bible, New International Version, Copyright © 1973, 1978, 1984 International Bible Society, used by permission of Zondervan Bible Publishers [NIV]. The other translation cited is the Living Bible [LB].

An effort has been made to locate sources and obtain permission where necessary for the quotations used in this book. In the event of any unintentional omission, a modification will gladly be incorporated in future printings.

ISBN 0-8499-8490-4
Printed in the United States of America

COVER DESIGN: Gary Lett
COVER PHOTOGRAPH: Phil Fewsmith

CONTENTS

Chuck first presented this series to his congregation in 1985 and Insight for Living aired it in 1986. In preparation of a new guide in 1994, preceding our airing the series, the coauthor of the guide, Bryce Klabunde, felt some of the titles needed to be altered to reflect more accurately the content of the sermons. On several occasions during this series, Chuck had been unable to complete his message so he had carried over portions of his outline to the next sermon along with adding some additional material. Sermon titles had been determined prior to these Sunday experiences and had never been changed.

If you currently have the 1986 cassette series and if you were to compare titles, you may have become confused with these changes, so hopefully the following information will help. The sermons are the same as originally presented, only four of the titles have been changed.

"Ages and Stages of Growing Up" (GUF 1B, 1986) was changed to "Growing Up in God's Family" because Chuck did not address the stages of growing up until the next message (GUF 2A).

"Birth and Infancy: Operation Survival" (GUF 2A, 1986) was changed to "Ages and Stages of Growing Up" because Chuck primarily covered the stages of growing up, with an introduction to birth and infancy.

"Let's Return to the Basics" (GUF 2B, 1986) was changed to "Birth and Infancy: Survival Basics" because Chuck covers birth and infancy in greater detail, including the basics for both.

"The Delights and Dangers of Childhood" (GUF 3B, 1986) was changed to "The Delights of Childhood" because Chuck did not address the dangers of childhood until the next message (GUF 4A).

INTRODUCTION

There is an enormous difference between growing old in the Lord and growing *up* in Him. One is automatic and requires no effort at all . . . just aging. But the other is never automatic, or easy. It calls for personal discipline, continual determination, and spiritual desire. Churches are full of sleepy saints who are merely "logging time" in God's family. Where are those en route to maturity . . . the soldiers of the Cross . . . the followers of the Lamb?

These messages are designed to jolt us awake. They address some of the reasons many Christians have opted for a soft rocking chair instead of a rugged obstacle course. But they represent more than strong exhortations. You will find encouragement and motivation . . . even a few how-to ideas that will turn your lethargic yawn into a smile of fresh hope.

Press on!

Chuck Swindoll

PUTTING TRUTH
INTO ACTION

K nowledge apart from application falls short of God's desire for
His children. He wants us to apply what we learn so that we
will change and grow. This study guide was prepared with these
goals in mind. As you go through the following pages, we hope your
desire to discover biblical truth will grow as your understanding of
God's Word increases and that you will be encouraged to apply what
you've learned.

To assist you in your study, we've included a section called
Living Insights at the end of each lesson. These exercises will
challenge you to study further and to think of specific ways to put
your discoveries into action.

There are many ways to use this guide—in personal devotions,
group studies, discussions with friends and family, and Sunday school
classes. And, of course, it's an ideal study aid when you're listening
to its corresponding "Insight for Living" radio series.

To benefit most from this study guide, we would encourage you
to consider it a spiritual journal. That's why we've included space
in the Living Insights for recording your thoughts and discoveries.
We hope you'll return to those sections often for review and encouragement as you continue to grow in your walk with Christ.

Bryce Klabunde
Coauthor of Text
Author of Living Insights

GROWING UP IN GOD'S FAMILY

Chapter 1

ANALYSIS OF A CROP FAILURE

Mark 4:1–20

Early one morning, a farmer rides his tractor into his fields to inspect the crops. For months he's been tilling the soil, sowing the seed, and nourishing the land. Now it's harvest time.

As his tractor rattles along, he notices something unusual. Some plants have matured to their full height and are heavy with ripened fruit. Other plants stand at only half the normal size. Still others are not much bigger than they were in early spring, their pale leaves drooping to the ground.

Why did some plants burst forth with vigorous growth and others remain small? The farmer nurtured all of them in exactly the same way. What made the difference?

An observer of Christians might ask the same questions. Why, after years of hearing the same instruction, reproofs, and encouragement, do some grow and others remain stunted? Why is there such a variety of responses to spiritual nurture? Church leaders have been scratching their heads over these issues for centuries. Have you ever wondered why you shoot up sometimes and languish at others? How can you grow more consistently and hardily in your faith?

In this study, we'll explore some answers to these questions. To begin, let's don our overalls and do what any farmer would do when some crops grow and some fail: analyze the soil. That's what Jesus did through a story He told one day to a vast crop of people who had gathered by the Sea of Galilee.

A Few Words about the Setting

They had come from all corners of the city and made such a large crowd that Jesus had to speak from a boat a little way offshore to be heard (Mark 4:1). He was teaching them in parables, which, according to William Barclay, were, and are, to be interpreted not

> phrase by phrase and word by word. They were spoken not to be studied at length and at leisure, but to produce an immediate impression and reaction. That is to say, *the parables must never be treated as allegories*. In an allegory every part and action and detail of the story has an inner significance. *The Pilgrim's Progress* and the *Faerie Queene* are allegories; in them every event and person and detail has a symbolic meaning. Clearly an allegory is something to be read and studied and examined; but a parable is something which was heard once and once only. Therefore what we must look for in a parable is not a situation in which every detail stands for something but a situation in which one great idea leaps out and shines like a flash of lightning.[1]

So, as you read Jesus' parable, imagine yourself sitting along the banks of the sea. Focus on His face and the words He is speaking. And watch for the great idea flashing through His parable of the sower and the soils.

A Close Look at the Parable

> "Listen to this! Behold, the sower went out to sow; and it came about that as he was sowing, some seed fell beside the road, and the birds came and ate it up. And other seed fell on the rocky ground where it did not have much soil; and immediately it sprang up because it had no depth of soil. And after the sun had risen, it was scorched; and because it had no root, it withered away. And other seed fell among the thorns, and the thorns came up and choked it, and it yielded no crop. And other seeds fell into the good soil and as they grew up and increased, they yielded a crop and produced thirty, sixty, and a hundredfold." And He was saying, "He who has ears to hear, let him hear." (Mark 4:3–9)

1. William Barclay, *The Gospel of Mark*, rev. ed., The Daily Study Bible Series (Philadelphia, Pa.: Westminster Press, 1975), p. 90.

The first seed fell "beside the road" on the *wayside soil*, where the farmer and his beast walked between the rows of plants. Because this soil was trodden on so regularly, it was packed hard. Scattered across this impenetrable surface, the seed had no chance to germinate. Instead, it became convenient breakfast food for passing birds.

Other seed fell on *stony soil*. According to William Barclay, Jesus may not have been referring to soil littered with stones, but

> a narrow skin of earth over a shelf of limestone rock. Much of Galilee was like that. In many fields the outcrop of the rock through the shallow soil could be seen. Seed which fell there germinated all right; but because the soil was so shallow and held so little nourishment and moisture, the heat of the sun soon withered the sprouting seed and it died.[2]

The sower also tossed some seed into *thorny soil*. Unlike the first two soils, which were so hard that the seeds could only rest on their surfaces, these next two soils actually allowed the seeds to penetrate deeply. However, although the thorny soil may have looked ready for seed because the weeds had been cut down or burned,

> below the surface the roots were still there; and in due time the weeds revived in all their strength. They grew with such rapidity and such virulence that they choked the life out of the seed.[3]

Finally, some seed fell into *fertile soil*. This ground received the seed into its nutrient-rich bed, nourishing it until it produced a bumper crop.

Now, what is the flash-of-lightning truth in Jesus' story? It's certainly more than "Watch where you throw your seed." Thankfully, Jesus Himself interprets the parable to help us grasp its meaning.

An Accurate Interpretation of the Story

Jesus begins by explaining that the seed is "the word" (v. 14). The sower, then, would be any messenger who spreads the principles of God's Word. And the remainder of Jesus' explanation answers

2. Barclay, *The Gospel of Mark*, p. 95.
3. Barclay, *The Gospel of Mark*, p. 96.

the questions we started this lesson with. So here is the central truth of the parable: the reason people respond differently to the same message is *the varying conditions of their hearts.* Let's examine each of the conditions more closely.

The Unresponsive Heart

The wayside soil represents people with unresponsive hearts. Jesus says,

> "And these are the ones who are beside the road where the word is sown; and when they hear, immediately Satan comes and takes away the word which has been sown in them." (v. 15)

Like grains of rice on concrete, God's Word only rests on top of these people's hearts. Nothing the messenger says penetrates the surface and convinces them of their need for a life-changing, personal relationship with God. They may attend church or hang around Christians, but because they are hardened to the truth, the Adversary easily picks off whatever morsels of the gospel land in their minds. As a result, they remain unrepentant and unsaved.

The Impulsive Heart

The rocky soil represents people with impulsive hearts. Jesus continues,

> "In a similar way these are the ones on whom seed was sown on the rocky places, who, when they hear the word, immediately receive it with joy; and they have no firm root in themselves, but are only temporary; then, when affliction or persecution arises because of the word, immediately they fall away." (vv. 16–17)

These people instantly respond to the truth because it wraps them in a blanket of warm feelings. They enjoy listening to feel-good sermons and singing their favorite church songs, but when the heat of affliction or persecution bears down on them, they shed God's words of life like bulky wool clothes. They, too, remain unsaved.

The Preoccupied Heart

Illustrating the people with preoccupied hearts is the thorny soil. According to Jesus,

"Others are the ones on whom seed was sown among the thorns; these are the ones who have heard the word, and the worries of the world, and the deceitfulness of riches, and the desires for other things enter in and choke the word, and it becomes unfruitful."[4] (vv. 18–19)

These people receive Christ into hearts that are already crowded with the roots of a thorny past. Soon after salvation, those old habits and thought patterns begin sprouting, but instead of digging them out by the roots, they try to live with them.

Jesus identifies three weedlike preoccupations. First, weighing down these believers' minds are "the worries of the world." Anxieties about the economy, the crime rate, health, or relationships wrap around their hearts, squeezing out joy and strangling faith.

Second, "the deceitfulness of riches" entangles some of these Christians who swallow the advertising line that happiness comes in a shrink-wrap package. This deception doesn't just ensnarl the rich; the cords of materialism wind around anyone who commits his or her life to pursuing money and possessions.

Jesus picks out the third preoccupation as "the desires for other things." He purposely leaves this one nonspecific, opening the gate to a broad field of weeds. Any desire that chokes out a believer's passion for Christ and shifts his or her priorities falls into this category.

For these Christians, nothing is wrong with the seed that has been sown in their lives. They've received the correct amount of nutrients, sun, and rain. But unfortunately, the worries and lures of this world have stunted their growth. The result is unfruitfulness.

The Productive Heart

The final soil condition in Jesus' parable represents productive hearts. These Christians hear, receive, and respond to the seed planted within them. They weed out any thorns that crop up. And, as a result, the seeds grow unhindered, bearing fruit in varying degrees: "thirty, sixty, and a hundredfold" (v. 20).

4. The Greek word for *choke* is also used in Matthew 18:28 referring to seizing a person by the throat to strangle him and again in Mark 5:13 referring to drowning.

An Honest Response to the Message

Like all good parables, Jesus' story begs a question: Which soil illustrates your heart? By evaluating your present spiritual condition, you're taking the first step toward growing up in God's family—which is the goal of our study. Is the soil of your life hard and unresponsive to the seed? Or is it impulsive and, to be honest, shallow? If so, the solution is simple. You don't need to work harder or attend church more often. Jesus says,

> "Truly, truly, I say to you, he who hears My word, and believes Him who sent Me, has eternal life, and does not come into judgment, but has passed out of death into life." (John 5:24)

Trust Christ for salvation. Surrender your life to Him. And receive His power to grow.

Maybe you've already received that power, but thorns are strangling your growth. Worries are distracting you, riches are deceiving you, and desires are taking charge of your life. Your prayers seem hypocritical, and you can't even remember your last meaningful quiet time with the Lord.

We encourage you to do two things. First, confess. Tell the Lord and, perhaps, a fellow believer that you've been distracted, deceived, and victimized by the weeds in your heart. No alcoholic, for example, has ever loosened the stranglehold of addiction without first admitting: "I'm an alcoholic." Healing begins with confession.

Then, repent. Repentance is the lengthy process of pulling up sin's weeds in your heart one by one, roots and all. Daily, invite the Spirit to sink His shovel of truth into your life and turn over everything your eyes see, your ears hear, and your lips speak. Over time, the penetrating rays of Christ's sun will cleanse you more and more, and His seed will produce a bounty of fruit, ready for harvest.

 Living Insights STUDY ONE

God's messengers have sown more seed in this century than ever before. So often, though, it tumbles down the wayside or scatters across a stone ledge or lodges itself among the thorns. How rare and wonderful is the fertile soil that gives it life.

Perhaps right now you're experiencing the spiritual growth that the fertile soil bears; or possibly your growth has been erratic and thorn-ridden; or maybe the seed is still lying dormant in your heart. Whatever your situation, this study is for you.

To get the most out of it, though, we encourage you to do one thing right at the beginning: loosen up the soil. Break up some of the clods of pride in your heart, dig up some hardened attitudes, and prepare your heart for change. The seed must have room to sink its roots. Are you willing to let it work its way through your life?

In the following space, take a few moments to express to the Lord your willingness to grow. You may want to confess something we pointed out in the lesson that may be choking your growth. Use the time to prepare yourself to receive His seed.

_____

_____

_____

_____

_____

_____

_____

 *Living Insights*

In the remainder of this study guide, we'll compare spiritual growth to growing up in a family. Specifically, we'll examine four stages of life: birth and infancy, childhood, adolescence, and adulthood. To help you begin thinking in these terms, write down a few of the characteristics of these stages of physical growth. Also, note some of the needs a person might have in each stage and how those needs are met.

Birth and Infancy

Characteristics: _____

_____

_____

Needs: _____

_____

_____

Childhood

Characteristics: _____

_____

_____

Needs: _____

_____

_____

Adolescence

Characteristics: _____

_____

_____

Needs: _____

_____

_____

Adulthood

Characteristics: _____

_____

_____

Needs: _____

_____

_____

Chapter 2

GROWING UP
IN GOD'S FAMILY

Selected Scriptures

J ust because you're grown doesn't mean you're *grown up*. For instance, an eighth grader who stretches the measuring tape to 6 feet 10 inches may be tall enough to play professional basketball; but pit him against a seasoned NBA player, and there's little doubt who would win. The teenager may be grown, but as an athlete he is not grown up.

What is true in the gym is also true in the church. A Christian may be an adult in size and appearance, but that doesn't mean he or she is spiritually grown up. How can we tell? Some of the marks of maturity are

- wisdom, not just knowledge

- self-discipline

- commitment to walk with Christ seven days a week

- determination to obey God and His Word no matter what the cost

- the ability to nourish oneself through personal Bible study

- compassion to care for others in need

- willingness to share responsibilities

- a contagious, positive lifestyle

The place where maturity is best developed is the same for believers as it is for an eighth grader—within the nurturing context of a family. And God's family is the church. Let's explore this metaphor in more detail.

The Church as a Family

Through the years, people have pictured the church in a variety of ways. Some imagine it as a corporation, complete with organizational charts and production quotas. Others see it as a hospital, a place to help the hurting and strengthen the weak. Because education is at the core of the church's calling, many have thought of it as a school. But the New Testament chooses another image to describe the church: a body (1 Cor. 12:12–27). As Christ's ears or eyes or feet, we each have specialized gifts and abilities that are necessary for a church to function in a healthy manner.

Equally important in the New Testament is the image of family. Although the church is never directly referred to as a family, the metaphor does peek out of several passages.

Scriptural Support

Paul's qualifications for church leaders hinge on an unexpected point:

> [An overseer] must be one who manages his own household well, keeping his children under control with all dignity (but if a man does not know how to manage his own household, how will he take care of the church of God?). (1 Tim. 3:4–5)

If the church was like a corporation, Paul probably would have recommended a look at the person's business, right? Instead, he says that good household leaders make good church leaders, implying that the church is more like a family.

Augmenting this point is the language often used to describe Christ's followers. For example,

> all who are being led by the Spirit of God, these are *sons* of God. For you have not received a spirit of slavery leading to fear again, but you have received a spirit of *adoption as sons* by which we cry out, "*Abba! Father!*" The Spirit Himself bears witness with our spirit that we are *children of God*. (Rom. 8:14–16, emphasis added)

God doesn't think of us as business clients or team members; He calls us His children—

> and if children, heirs also, heirs of God and fellow heirs with Christ, if indeed we suffer with Him in order that we may also be glorified with Him. (v. 17)

Also, if we all have the same heavenly Father, then we must be brothers and sisters. Paul specifically writes,

[We] are of God's household, having been built upon the foundation of the apostles and prophets, Christ Jesus Himself being the corner stone. (Eph. 2:19b–20)

The roots of our family tree go all the way down to the apostles, prophets, and Jesus Christ Himself. What a rich heritage!

Practical Significance

Thinking of ourselves as a family naturally leads to considering what it means to live like a family. Let's look at some of the practical implications of this perspective.

First, *we are family members, not isolated strangers*. Granted, families are not always loving—what brother or sister can't remember squabbling over whose turn it was to do the dishes or fighting in the backseat because "he's touching me!" Yet despite the friction, there is usually a bond between siblings that lasts through the years. Idyllic relationships don't exist in most families, but woven throughout the sometimes fraying fabric are threads of commitment that hold everyone together. People can be themselves. No one is a stranger. Prejudices are quickly swept out the back door. Rank, title, or class distinction aren't important. The same should be true in the church family.

Second, *we are to relate to each other as family members*. In a healthy family, the members are supportive, encouraging, and mutually involved in one another's lives. The same is also true of the church, as Paul wrote to the Galatian believers:

> So then, while we have opportunity, let us do good to all men, and *especially to those who are of the household of the faith*. (Gal. 6:10, emphasis added)

Another important aspect of family life is a willingness to follow the leadership of those in authority. How many nerves have been frayed and relationships strained by those who treat others with disregard and contentiously kick at trustworthy authority? Christ would not have it that way in the family—nor in His church.

> Obey your leaders, and submit to them; for they keep watch over your souls, as those who will give an account. Let them do this with joy and not with grief, for this would be unprofitable for you. (Heb. 13:17)

One last facet of families is the responsibility to uphold the family name. Just as our character, behavior, and integrity influence people's opinion of our earthly family, so they reflect on our heavenly Father and His eternal family. We represent Him to the world, which is both a tremendous privilege and a humbling responsibility; nevertheless, it is a task inspiring the highest praise.

> To Him be the glory *in the church* and in Christ Jesus to all generations forever and ever. Amen. (Eph. 3:21, emphasis added; see also 1 Thess. 2:12)

Relating to each other as members of a family provides a nurturing atmosphere for growing up, but we must not forget the third and most important factor: *We are responsible for our own growth.* Mom and Dad can provide a healthy climate to grow in, but as we get older it's up to us to keep stretching and developing. In the same way, each Christian must personally determine to climb the sometimes difficult trail toward maturity in Christ.

Some, however, believe that continued immaturity is excusable. After all, they're only human, and it's natural to settle back into the comforts of childish behavior. Other Christians think maturity is strictly up to God. They think it will somehow come automatically, without any effort or discipline on their part.

Both attitudes result in Christians who should be adults but are still spiritual babies. The writer to the Hebrews addressed a group of thumb-sucking adults:

> For though by this time you ought to be teachers, you have need again for someone to teach you the elementary principles of the oracles of God, and you have come to need milk and not solid food. For everyone who partakes only of milk is not accustomed to the word of righteousness, for he is a babe. But solid food is for the mature, who because of practice have their senses trained to discern good and evil. (Heb. 5:12–14; see also 1 Cor. 3:1–3)

Perhaps you've been on a milk diet since you became a Christian. Something inside you, though, longs for some juicy spiritual steaks. That desire may be God's prompting to not just grow but to grow up. Here are a few questions to help you search your heart.

The Issues and Questions Family Members Must Face

Where am I now? This question touches on the issue of

identification—identifying your present level of maturity. Are you a newborn baby in the faith? A child? An adolescent? An adult? In the next chapter, we'll help you examine more specifically your stage of growth.

What will it take to dislodge me from my present stage and accelerate growth? This is the issue of change—a process that is never easy. It may mean getting serious about determining your direction in life or confronting negative habits. It may require you to stop making the same old excuses and start investing your energy in growth. What will it take to mature?

When do I plan to start? This concerns the issue of urgency. G. K. Chesterton was once asked what single book he would most like to have with him were he stranded on a desert island. The interviewer may have been expecting the title of some lofty, philosophical book, but Chesterton, with characteristic wit, replied: "Thomas's *Guide to Practical Shipbuilding.*"[1]

Perhaps you feel like you're going around in circles on an island of spiritual routine. You don't need a lot of philosophy; you need to get your hands on something practical so you can get off the island and start your voyage toward maturity in Christ. In the chapters ahead, we hope to give you the shipbuilding tools necessary. But growing up is, ultimately, up to you. Won't you plan to start today?

 Living Insights

Just as plants grow best in fertile soil, we mature best spiritually in the rich soil of God's family. In the lesson, we discussed three characteristics of relating as members of God's family. Let's sink our roots into those characteristics and apply them to our lives.

First, family members are supportive, encouraging, and mutually involved. Using the early church as a model, look up the following verses and write down how history's first Christians expressed these qualities.

Acts 2:41–47 _____

_____

---

1. G. K. Chesterton, as quoted in *The Little, Brown Book of Anecdotes,* ed. Clifton Fadiman (Boston, Mass.: Little, Brown and Co., 1985), p. 117.

Acts 21:3–6 _____

_____

2 Corinthians 8:1–5 _____

_____

Allowing their example to stir your thinking, how can you show these qualities to someone in God's family this week?

_____

_____

_____

Second, family members show willingness to follow authority. By nature, we tend to buck authority, desiring a free rein to roam wherever we want to go. According to Hebrews 13:17, what are some reasons to willingly follow our spiritual leaders?

_____

_____

Have you been a source of joy for your leaders? How would you measure your willingness to follow them?

_____

_____

In the next Living Insights, we'll address the third characteristic of relating as members of God's family: upholding the family name.

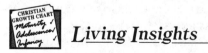

Living Insights

STUDY TWO

What's in a name? A lot. In his book *Wishful Thinking*, Frederick Buechner explains the inner significance of a name.

> [Buechner] is my name. It is pronounced Beekner. If somebody mispronounces it in some foolish way, I have the feeling that what's foolish is me. If somebody forgets it, I feel that it's I who am

forgotten. . . . If my name were different, I would be different. When I tell somebody my name, I have given him a hold over me that he didn't have before. If he calls it out, I stop, look, and listen whether I want to or not.

In the Book of Exodus, God tells Moses that his name is Yahweh, and God hasn't had a peaceful moment since.[2]

God wants us to call out His name, but He doesn't want us to trample it underfoot. According to the fourth commandment:

"You shall not take the name of the Lord your God in vain, for the Lord will not leave him unpunished who takes His name in vain." (Exod. 20:7)

God takes His name seriously. Notice from the following verses all He does "for His name's sake." Write down the things you observe.

Psalm 23:3 _____

Psalm 25:11 _____

Psalm 31:3 _____

Psalm 79:9 _____

Because He is our Father, we must bear His name with honor. When we exhibit spiritual maturity, we hold His name up high. But when we stumble into a pit of sin, we drag His divine name through the mud with us.

According to Matthew 19:29, what does Jesus promise those who commit themselves to Him, for His name's sake?

_____

What's in a name? In the Lord's name, there's a universe of love and power and justice. So,

whatever you do in word or deed, do all in the name of the Lord Jesus. (Col. 3:17a)

2. Frederick Buechner, *Wishful Thinking: A Theological ABC* (New York, N.Y.: Harper and Row, Publishers, 1973), p. 12.

Chapter 3

AGES AND STAGES OF GROWING UP

Selected Scriptures

Growing up doesn't happen all at once; it comes in stages, just like our physical growth. From a pudgy baby to a willowy child to a sturdy adult, we can see the gradual movement toward maturity. Our mental capacities develop in phases also, from a child's simple understanding to an adult's ability to ponder the universe. Certainly, we all go through stages of emotional growth. Children can't cope with stress like adults can, and we wouldn't expect them to—just as we wouldn't expect a two-year-old boy to suddenly grow whiskers or a second-grade girl to comprehend quantum physics.

What is true physically, mentally, and emotionally is also true spiritually. We can't expect new believers to be as discerning and wise as mature believers. They must grow up in stages also— unhurried, allowed to mature at their own pace. Let's take a few moments to browse through the stages of spiritual growth, picking out the prominent characteristics of each one.

The Ages and Stages of Growing Up			
	Description	*Statement*	*Focus*
Birth/Infancy	Immaturity	"Help Me!"	Surviving
Childhood	Discovery	"Tell Me!"	Learning
Adolescence	Irresponsibility	"Show Me!"	Challenging
Adulthood	Maturity	"Follow Me!"	Serving

The first stage is *birth and infancy*. Newborn babies are fragile, dependent, innocent, and completely incapable of discerning danger. They would just as readily grab a red-hot poker as a baby rattle. In the same way, indiscriminating infant Christians will often grab for appealing false teaching, not realizing the risk. Believers in this stage cry out, "Help me!" Just surviving is their main focus. And until they begin to walk on their own, more mature Christians must spoon-feed them God's Word and give them constant attention.

In the second stage, *childhood*, the focus is learning. Believers in this phase are just beginning to feed themselves God's truths, and their joy of discovery is electric. "Tell me!" is their cry, and their energy and curiosity seem boundless. The danger, however, is that they are very impressionable and their discernment is limited. Easily persuaded, they can be tempted to follow any strong authority figure. This stage eventually ends when they are able to reproduce their faith in others.

The third stage is *adolescence*. Believers passing through this phase are capable of reproducing their faith but are sometimes reluctant to do so. Their level of discernment is not always reliable, and they are often critical of others yet unwilling to contribute anything themselves. They focus on challenging others, saying, "Show me!" or, "Prove it to me!" They don't settle for pat answers and "the way things have always been"; instead, they challenge us to rethink our beliefs and prove the integrity of our lives. They are often idealistic, intolerant, and independent. When they eventually shift their focus to the needs of others, they are ready to enter the next level.

Stage four is *adulthood*. This is a period of stability and balance. Adult Christians can easily spot a spiritual fraud because they have developed great discernment (see Heb. 5:14). With their focus on serving others, their cry is "Follow me!" as they follow Christ. They don't grasp at every Christian fad that breezes by. They know maturity is a lengthy process that requires what Friedrich Nietzsche termed a "long obedience in the same direction."[1]

Christian thinker Eugene Peterson observed the need for this rare quality in our prepackaged, consumer world:

> It is not difficult in such a world to get a person interested in the message of the gospel; it is terrifically difficult to sustain the interest. Millions of people in our culture make decisions for Christ, but there is a dreadful attrition rate. Many claim to have been born again, but the evidence for mature Christian discipleship is slim. In our kind of culture anything, even news about God, can be sold if it is packaged freshly; but when it loses its novelty, it goes on the garbage heap. There is a great market for religious

1. Friedrich Nietzsche, as quoted by Eugene H. Peterson in *A Long Obedience in the Same Direction* (Downers Grove, Ill.: InterVarsity Press, 1980), p. 9.

experience in our world; there is little enthusiasm for the patient acquisition of virtue, little inclination to sign up for a long apprenticeship in what earlier generations of Christians called holiness.[2]

In this study, we want to guide you to sign up for that long apprenticeship under Christ. We want to help you say to the Father, "Here's my life, Lord. Shape me into the kind of person You want me to be. And don't stop changing me until I am carrying my share of the world mission You have in mind for Your children." That's what growing up is all about.

The Place Where We All Begin

We all begin our journeys at the very same place—birth. No one is born more mature than anyone else. Can you imagine one newborn baby suddenly standing up and walking around while the others aren't even able to turn over in the crib? Newborn believers begin their spiritual lives at the same maturity level as well. We are all born untrained, inexperienced, and a little unsure of our new spiritual world.

The Fact of Birth

According to the apostle John, a person is spiritually born when he or she personally trusts Christ for salvation.

> But as many as received Him, to them He gave the right to become children of God, even to those who believe in His name, who were born not of blood, nor of the will of the flesh, nor of the will of man, but of God. (John 1:12–13)

People aren't automatically born into God's family just because their parents are Christians or they belong to a certain denomination. Some religious people may assume they are Christians because they try to follow the Golden Rule. But as Jesus told the rule-keeping Pharisee Nicodemus,

> "Truly, truly, I say to you, unless one is born again, he cannot see the kingdom of God." (3:3)

2. Peterson, A Long Obedience, p. 12.

Just as we must be born physically to become a member of our earthly family, so we must be born spiritually to become a child of God. At the moment a person believes in Jesus Christ, he or she emerges from the womb into eternal life (v. 16). Then comes infancy.

The Reality of Infancy

Jesus alludes to the importance of this period, saying to His disciples:

> "Truly I say to you, unless you are converted and become like children, you shall not enter the kingdom of heaven. Whoever then humbles himself as this child, he is the greatest in the kingdom of heaven." (Matt. 18:3–4)

Is Jesus telling adults to become like little children? This seems strange to us because we tend to think of babies as helpless and incapable. Yet Jesus sees the childlike virtues of humility and innocent trust as essential for growing up spiritually healthy.

Peter also observed the value of infancy. He told his adult readers:

> Like newborn babes, long for the pure milk of the word, that by it you may grow in respect to salvation. (1 Pet. 2:2)

Few scenes are as touching as a tiny baby cradled in a mother's arms, drawing nourishment from her breast. Equally heartwarming is watching an infant believer being suckled by God's Word through pure, biblical teaching. Maturing Christians must never wean themselves off that source of nourishment.

And neither must churches. The milk of God's truth was all the three thousand members of the very first church had to sustain them. They had no building, no background in theology, no history, and no written New Testament. So, like newborn babies longing for mother's milk,

> they were continually devoting themselves to the apostles' *teaching* and to fellowship, to the breaking of bread and to prayer. (Acts 2:42, emphasis added)

The Lifestyle of the Newborn

If you've been a Christian for a long time, it can be hard to remember what infancy in Christ was like and what a baby believer's needs are. So let's spend some time refreshing our memory.

What Is It Like?

Babies in general all share certain characteristics.

- They need a great deal of time and hands-on attention.

- They require constant supervision for safety reasons.

- They're totally dependent on others to feed them, clean them, and keep them on schedule.

- They have a short attention span and need continual repetition of the basics, like, "Hot!" and, "No-no" and, "Off limits."

In a sense, these characteristics are true of newborn believers too. Adult Christians must spend a lot of time with them, keeping them safe from old sinful patterns, gently correcting their mistakes, feeding them truth, and reminding them of the boundaries.

As challenging as the labor of parenting baby believers is, the excitement makes it more than worthwhile.

What Makes This So Exciting?

Three things in particular make infancy shine with excitement. First, *rapid growth occurs during this stage*. Think of the many changes that take place in a baby's first year. She learns to smile, follow you with her eyes, turn over, sit up, clap hands, say a word or two, eat from a spoon, and crawl all over the place! Baby Christians grow rapidly too; every week they learn something new or make a subtle change. Before you know it, they're walking.

Second, *they have an uncomplicated innocence and simplicity of life*. There's something fresh and real about new Christians' first prayers, for example. They haven't learned any religious jargon; they tend to talk to God in a more natural way. "Well, God," a new believer might pray, "hope you're listening. Thanks for caring about me." Like a parent hearing a baby's first words, the Lord must delight in these kinds of prayers.

Third, *the new believer exudes total trust*. As a young child un-hesitatingly jumps from the edge of the pool into his dad's waiting arms, so young Christians leap without worry into the arms of Christ. This childlike faith is a precious quality, having brought them to salvation (see Mark 10:15).

What Are the Dangers?

Bundled with the excitement of a person's nascent faith, however, are some potential dangers. Because new believers lack spiritual discernment, they are easy targets for smooth-talking cultists or extremists who subtly twist the Scripture. Also, young, enthusiastic Christians can be given too much responsibility too soon, their eagerness taken advantage of at a time when they are simply incapable of handling the load.

Essentials for Surviving Those Early Years

Because we want to protect new Christians from these perils, here are a few ABCs for surviving the early years of faith.

A *Affection and affirmation.* New believers require lots of patient, tender loving care.

B *Basics of the Christian life.* They need to know how to pray, how to read the Bible, and how to please God. And they need wise counsel to keep their balance and avoid extremes.

C *Compassion, care, and courtesy.* When they spill a glass of milk or fall down and scrape their knees, they don't need lectures. They need understanding and warmth.

D *Diet of biblical nourishment.* Learning how to feed oneself the truths of God's Word is essential. New Christians may make a few messes trying to interpret and apply the Bible, but that's OK. It's all a part of growing up.

 Living Insights STUDY ONE

In the previous chapter, we mentioned the importance of identifying your stage of spiritual development. Now that we've overviewed the four stages, take a moment to determine which one you're in right now and place a check beside it.

❑ Birth and Infancy

❑ Childhood

❑ Adolescence

❑ Adulthood

What characteristics of your Christian walk indicate that you are in this stage?

_____

_____

_____

_____

If you are in the birth and infancy stage, maybe you wish you could be like the more mature Christians around you. Perhaps you're frustrated because you want to grow up faster. If so, relax. It's OK to not know how to run when you're just learning to walk. Instead, focus on some of the positive traits of your new faith. From the lesson, pick out a few exciting characteristics of your life with God. Write them down in the following space and thank the Lord for helping you grow in His time and in His way. For as Paul wrote,

> I am confident of this very thing, that He who began a good work in you will perfect it until the day of Christ Jesus. (Phil. 1:6)

_____

_____

_____

If you are in one of the other stages of spiritual growth, what has been your attitude lately toward infant believers? Have you been a little impatient? Perhaps critical of their mistakes? If so, what can you say to baby believer friends that will encourage them? And what can you do to protect them from some of the dangers we explored?

_____

_____

_____

Over the years, has your childlike trust lost itself in a swirling tide of disappointment or fear? Perhaps a scene from Frederick Buechner's novel *The Wizard's Tide* will help you retrieve your innocent faith.[3]

Mr. Schroeder has decided that his son, Teddy, is old enough to swim out with him to some barrels anchored a way offshore. Halfway to the barrels, Teddy starts getting nervous.

> Teddy thought the barrels still looked a long way off, and the beach was so far behind he could hardly recognize his mother and Bean [Teddy's sister] sitting on it. His arms were beginning to ache, and he was feeling out of breath. What if he started to drown, he thought? What if he called for help and his father, who was a little ahead of him, didn't hear? What if a giant octopus swam up from below and wrapped him in its slimy green tentacles?
>
> But just as he was thinking these things, his father turned around and treaded water, waiting for him.
>
> "How about a lift the rest of the way?" Mr. Schroeder said. So Teddy paddled over and put his arms around his father's neck from behind, and that was the best part of the day for him and the part he remembered for many years afterward. . . .
>
> His mother said bad things about his father. She said that he had no get-up-and-go and that he was worse than Grandpa Schroeder already though thirty years younger. She said he needed a swift kick in the pants and things like that. And Teddy knew that his father did things that he wished he wouldn't, like drink too many cocktails and drive his car up on the lawn and come to kiss him and Bean goodnight with his face all clammy and cold.
>
> But as he swam out toward the barrels on his

---

3. This Living Insight is adapted from the study guide *He Gave Gifts*, coauthored by Bryce Klabunde, from the Bible-teaching ministry of Charles R. Swindoll (Anaheim, Calif.: Insight for Living, 1992), pp. 86–87.

father's back, he also knew there was no place in the whole Atlantic ocean where he felt so safe.[4]

This image of a boy clinging to his daddy's shoulders aptly portrays the kind of childlike dependence on the Lord we need while swimming through the dangerous waters of our lives. If Teddy felt secure trusting in his often-failing father, how much more should we feel confident in our never-failing Lord? Surely, there is no other place in the whole world where we can feel so safe.

4. Frederick Buechner, *The Wizard's Tide* (San Francisco, Calif.: Harper and Row, Publishers, 1990), pp. 45–46.

Chapter 4

BIRTH AND INFANCY: SURVIVAL BASICS

Selected Scriptures

T he church is in the baby business, and we are the attending physicians. As obstetricians, we carefully monitor the progress of our non-Christian friends still living in the dark womb of unbelief. Anxiously, we listen for a faint heartbeat of hope. With a sensitive touch, we feel them turn and position themselves for delivery. Then we wait. At any time, labor may begin as the muscles of God's Spirit start pushing them toward the moment of decision.

Spiritual birth is not easy. The baby must descend through a narrow channel of faith, and, at first, the way seems impassable. But God is powerful, and we are present in the delivery room— watching, encouraging, preparing.

Finally, the moment of belief arrives, and out of the darkness the baby emerges into the light of eternal life. A child of God is born into our waiting hands.

Now we must assume a new role. The work of birth is over; the work of growth is just beginning. As pediatricians, we check the baby for a healthy delivery and start nourishing him or her with the pure milk of God's Word. Later we'll help the newborn learn the basics of life: how to eat, how to walk, how to talk. There's so much to do! Day by day, step by step, choice by choice, the child slowly matures into an adult.

A Reminder of the Ages and Stages of Growth

As we discovered in the previous chapter, the baby will go through several stages of growth en route to maturity. A helpful way to visualize this process is by imagining the spiral of a snail's shell.

Birth, of course, is the center point. The subsequent stages circle around the middle by means of an ever-increasing curve. Instead of hoisting ourselves up the stages by climbing distinct stair steps, we flow through the stages. They comprise a single unit, a continual path, and it is best to follow the path steadily and without hurry. Although we may vacillate between stages or even get stuck in one for years, the goal is the outer ring: adulthood. But even there, the pathway continues to curve, and we really never stop growing.

Ages and Stages
Toward Christian Maturity

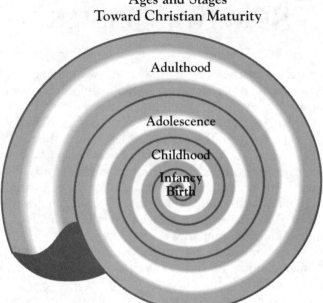

In order to journey to the goal of maturity, it's important to know where you're starting from. Imagine a big red X on the chart with the words You Are Here! underneath. Where would your X be located? In the infancy stage? The adolescent stage? Perhaps you're somewhere between stages.

Although we can't determine where you are for you, we can describe the stages. So, taking on the roles of obstetrician and pediatrician, let's turn to the "medical journal" of Scripture for some basics of spiritual birth and infancy.

A Return to the Basics of Spiritual Infancy

Chapter 1, page 1: Some basics about birth.

The Birth Basics

First, Scripture is clear that *you must be born from above.* Peter wrote to a group of people who had already experienced spiritual birth.

Notice how he refers to their birth as well as its heavenly benefits:

Blessed be the God and Father of our Lord Jesus Christ, who according to His great mercy has caused us to be born again to a living hope through the resurrection of Jesus Christ from the dead, to obtain an inheritance which is imperishable and undefiled and will not fade away, reserved in heaven for you, who are protected by the power of God through faith for a salvation ready to be revealed in the last time. (1 Pet. 1:3–5; see also v. 23)

Peter explains further that these "born again" people had received "salvation" (v. 9) and become "obedient children" (v. 14), because they were redeemed[1]

with precious blood, as of a lamb unblemished and spotless, the blood of Christ. (v. 19)

Those who have been born from above receive all these spiritual privileges in the same way that a newborn baby receives a birth certificate, a home, and a family. Some people, however, assume they own these birthrights, even though they've never actually been born again. Nicodemus was one man who thought he held a spiritual birth certificate because of his Jewish heritage and religious works. You may recall from the previous chapter that Jesus didn't mince words in pointing out his inner need:

"Truly, truly, I say to you, unless one is born again, he cannot see the kingdom of God." (John 3:3)

Jesus' statement takes Nicodemus off guard, snagging his seamless theological cloak. Perplexed, the Pharisee asks,

"How can a man be born when he is old? He cannot enter a second time into his mother's womb and be born, can he?" Jesus answered, "Truly, truly, I say to you, unless one is born of water and the Spirit, he cannot enter into the kingdom of God. That which

---

1. "The Greek words *lytroō* (usually translated 'redeem') and *apolytrōsis* ('redemption') are derived from *lytron* ('a ransom' or 'price of release'), which was almost a technical term in the ancient world for the purchase or manumission of a slave." John R. W. Stott, *The Cross of Christ* (Downers Grove, Ill.: InterVarsity Press, 1986), pp. 175–76. We were slaves to sin, standing naked and ashamed in the marketplace, when Jesus purchased us with the ransom price of His own blood.

is born of the flesh is flesh, and that which is born of the Spirit is spirit. Do not marvel that I said to you, 'You must be born again.' The wind blows where it wishes and you hear the sound of it, but do not know where it comes from and where it is going; so is everyone who is born of the Spirit." (vv. 4–8)

With each word Jesus speaks, Nicodemus' religious garb slowly unravels. He pleads,

"How can these things be?" Jesus answered and said to him, "Are you the teacher of Israel, and do not understand these things?" (vv. 9b–10)

The emphasis is on the definite article, "*the* teacher of Israel." When it comes to understanding and interpreting the Law, Nicodemus is the chief justice of Israel's Supreme Court. Yet, with all his religious knowledge, he can't comprehend spiritual birth. "It was outside of his groove," notes Greek scholar A. T. Robertson, who then quips: "Rote, rut, rot, the three terrible r's of mere traditionalism."[2]

So, for this sophisticated teacher of Israel, Jesus weaves together some plain words of truth so simple that, ironically, they've become the Sunday school primer for countless children:

"For God so loved the world, that He gave His only begotten Son, that whoever believes in Him should not perish, but have eternal life." (v. 16)

A second basic truth about spiritual birth is that it *must be biblical.* It must be God's way, not our way. According to Paul's letter to Titus:

He saved us, not on the basis of deeds which we have done in righteousness, but according to His mercy, by the washing of regeneration and renewing by the Holy Spirit, whom He poured out upon us richly through Jesus Christ our Savior. (3:5–6)

Babies bring nothing with them into this world; they're born naked and dependent. Similarly, the Bible says we must enter new

---

2. Archibald Thomas Robertson, *Word Pictures in the New Testament* (Grand Rapids, Mich.: Baker Book House, 1932), p. 47.

life stripped of every claim of personal righteousness, trusting Christ alone. That's God's way of salvation. Our way is to come to Him draped in silken church traditions, perfumed by religious accomplishments, and adorned with good works. Nicodemus came to Jesus that way, and Jesus told him he was still in the womb. He needed to be born again.

Third, *your birth must be personal.* Twins have never been born into the family of God. We are born one at a time, not paired up with a Christian brother or sister. We can't borrow someone else's faith or be born into heaven by means of a surrogate. Our faith must be our own.

Fourth, *your birth must be authentic.* Some people base their salvation on a "magic" prayer they once recited. But an authentic spiritual birth is not based on mere words; rather, it is based on the inner faith those words represent. Like wedding vows, prayers and rituals are meaningless unless we genuinely commit ourselves to what we're saying and to the Person we're saying them to.

The Growth Basics

In chapter 2 of our spiritual medical journal, we study pediatrics. Our newborns have to grow! There are four spiritual basics for growing up healthy, and here are three of them. The fourth we'll cover in the following chapter.

The first growth basic is *how to obey.* Remember what Peter called his born-again readers? "Obedient children" (1 Pet. 1:14a). One of the first things these infant believers had learned was that God's "no" meant "No!" His "stop" meant "Stop!" His "don't" meant "Don't!" Specifically, the Lord instructed them:

> Do not be conformed to the former lusts which were yours in your ignorance, but like the Holy One who called you, be holy yourselves also in all your behavior; because it is written, "You shall be holy, for I am holy." And if you address as Father the One who impartially judges according to each man's work, conduct yourselves in fear during the time of your stay upon earth. (vv. 14b–16)

These commands fall on the hearts of non-Christians like rain on tin roofs. They can't absorb them into their lives because they are hardened to God's Spirit. Peter's readers, too, were once unable to obey the Lord in their "ignorance." But now their hearts are like soft, green meadows, willingly soaking up His commands. The difference is, they've learned to trust God.

When we trust the Lord to know what is best for our lives, obedience naturally follows. For instance, children may be too young to understand the dangers of playing in the street, but their parents do. All children understand is that their parents love them, and that's all they need to know to obey.

What happens when God's children don't learn this growth basic? They end up dragging a resistant, disobedient attitude with them into childhood and adolescence. They'll never reach adulthood until they learn to trust and obey.

Second, infants must learn *how to eat*. Learning how to obey emphasizes the importance of trust; learning how to eat stresses the importance of proper nourishment. Babies choke on solid food. It frustrates them, and they eventually spit it out. But they long for a bottle of warm milk, and they'll gulp that down heartily. In the same way, spiritual infants "long for the pure milk of the word" (2:2). And their survival depends on a steady, nourishing diet of God's simple truths.

Not eating is one of the signs of a sick baby. When we're sick with worry or despair, our tendency is to push aside our spiritual milk. But, like Job, who despaired even of his life, we must also be able to say during the dark times:

"I have treasured the words of His mouth more
than my necessary food." (Job 23:12b)

A third growth basic is *how to talk*, emphasizing the importance of prayer. Peter advises us solemnly:

The end of all things is at hand; therefore, be of
sound judgment and sober spirit for the purpose of
prayer. (1 Pet. 4:7)

Sometimes we complicate prayer, dressing it up with sophisticated words and clichés that we never use in normal conversation. Essentially, though, prayer is just talking with God—anytime, anywhere.

New Christians may feel self-conscious in their first attempts to talk to God, imagining themselves as two-year-olds calling a cookie "kweekie" and a blanket "binkie." The heavenly Father, though, takes great pride in His infants when they talk to Him. It doesn't matter that they don't know all the "right" words. In fact, their prayers are often more meaningful because they come straight from the heart.

A Response from All Who Hear

As obstetricians, we need to ask you whether you've been born from above. If the answer is yes, it's time to move on to some pediatric questions: Have you mastered the basics of babyhood? Are you obeying? Eating? Talking? These are basics we never outgrow.

 Living Insights

Who can resist pausing to admire the Golden Gate Bridge? Its two pillars tower high above the churning Pacific like twin guardians of the San Francisco Bay. Cascading like streamers from the iron-red pillars, the cables trail out of the clouds to support the arching roadway below. You'd think the lines would snap in the stiff wind, yet they dance defiantly above the water, giving the bridge both elegance and tenacious strength.

Like any bridge, though, the Golden Gate is nothing more than a way to get from point A to point B. Its stately form is meaningless apart from its practical function. If, for some reason, it stopped ten feet short of one side, it would cease to be a bridge. It would be useless.

If you're trying to walk to heaven on the bridge of tradition and religious good works, the Bible clearly warns you that no matter how elaborate and sturdy the bridge may seem, it stops short because of sin. "For all have sinned," wrote the apostle Paul, "and fall short of the glory of God" (Rom. 3:23).

Only one bridge spans the distance from earth to heaven.

> For there is one God, and one mediator also between God and men, the man Christ Jesus, who gave Him-self as a ransom for all, the testimony borne at the proper time. (1 Tim. 2:5–6)

What bridge have you been trusting to lead you to heaven? Can it be that, like Nicodemus, you've been relying on your religious heritage and moral goodness? Your bridge may be beautiful; people may even pause and admire it. But it is useless.

If you've never personally trusted Christ, now is the time to

31

cross His bridge to salvation. Confess your self-reliance, accept His complete forgiveness of your sins, and tell Him you believe in Him alone for your salvation. We've provided you some space to record your thoughts and express your faith to the Lord.[3]

_____

_____

_____

_____

_____

 Living Insights

Picture Albert Einstein teaching math to kindergartners. Or Van Cliburn giving piano lessons to a six-year-old. Or Babe Ruth coaching a T-ball team. Hard to imagine, isn't it?

Now think about Jesus, the Son of God, showing us how to live a holy life. That's even harder to imagine, but it really happened. Stepping down from His divine throne, Jesus entered our kindergarten classroom as our teacher. He sat beside us on the piano bench, placing His hands on ours. And He wrapped His arms around us to help us steady our baseball bat. He became one of us to show us the basics.

From the following verses, what are some of the ways Jesus showed us to obey the Father?

Matthew 26:38–39 _____

John 4:31–34; 17:4 _____

John 13:3–15 _____

From this next set of verses, in what ways did Jesus show us how to nourish ourselves with the Word?

Matthew 4:1–11 _____

3. Your new faith in Christ draws you near to God as His precious child and secures your future in heaven (see John 1:12; Eph. 1:13). Let us help you grow. Please write our Counseling Department at Post Office Box 69000, Anaheim, California 92817-0900 for encouragement and information.

Luke 2:41–47 _____

And from these verses, how did Jesus model talking to God?

Matthew 6:5–15 _____

Matthew 14:23 _____

Mark 6:46 _____

We spend our lives learning and relearning these basics. Don't feel frustrated if you just don't seem to get them right. Pick one and work on it for a while. Your Teacher is more than willing to show you how.

Chapter 5

LOOK . . . I'M WALKING!

Ephesians 5:1–8, 15–21

Honey, get the camera! Hurry! *Now!*"

Upstairs, the husband is dressing in the bedroom when he hears his wife's urgent call. With his pants halfway on, he frantically pogo sticks down the hall, trying to insert his other foot through the flapping pants leg.

"Hurrryyy!" she cries. "You're going to miss seeing the baby's first steps!"

By the time he reaches the top of the stairs, he has his pants on and is fumbling with the buttons as he skids down the steps. Still running, he lands at the bottom, hotfoots it over some scattered toys in the kitchen, and slides into the family room, panting.

His wife is sitting on the floor, her legs in a V and her arms extended toward the wobbly one-year-old standing a few feet away. Grabbing the video camera out of the closet, he throws off the lens cover and aims. "Rolling!"

The baby grins at her silly daddy squinting behind the funny-looking box.

"Come to Mommy," prompts the mother. "C'mon, sweetie."

Her eyes flashing determination, the baby shifts her delicate balance and takes a small step. Then another and another and another.

"She's doing it! She's doing it!" cheer Mom and Dad. The baby squeals and laughs, her bright, round eyes seeming to announce, "Look . . . I'm walking!"

◆

A baby's first steps. It's one of those moments in life parents go gaga over. Can you imagine, then, how thrilled our heavenly Father must be as he watches us take our first spiritual steps? Like an earthly parent, He, too, waits with arms outstretched and cheers us on with coaxing encouragement. Let's listen now to some of His steadying words.

Walking: An Understanding of the Term

To help balance the wobbly legs of His children, God has given us solid ideas of what it means to walk spiritually.

> But I say, walk by the Spirit, and you will not carry out the desire of the flesh. (Gal. 5:16)

> Walk in a manner worthy of the Lord, to please Him in all respects, bearing fruit in every good work and increasing in the knowledge of God. (Col. 1:10)

> As you therefore have received Christ Jesus the Lord, so walk in Him. (2:6)

> Walk in a manner worthy of the God who calls you into His own kingdom and glory. (1 Thess. 2:12)

These verses each reveal what keeps us on our feet—a purpose that we can lean on; namely, to walk in such a way that brings glory to God. To reach that goal, our Father has stationed some signposts in Scripture to point us in the right direction. But He doesn't stop there. He not only shows us His path, He tells us how to walk in it.

Walking: An Explanation of the Process

Before examining more closely the how-tos of walking, it's important to remember that falling down is a part of the learning process. How wonderful it would be to stroll along perfectly the first time on our feet as Christians. But, like children, we begin with a few wavering baby steps, then we toddle awhile, holding other Christians' hands. Only later do we learn to run with grace. And never do we walk just by reading a manual or watching an instructional video. We learn by doing and practicing.

Initial Commands

Helping us know what to do first, Paul begins with some commands about our Christian walk.

> Therefore be imitators of God, as beloved children; and walk in love, just as Christ also loved you, and gave Himself up for us, an offering and a sacrifice to God as a fragrant aroma. (Eph. 5:1–2)

Because we're God's children, we long to mimic the Lord just as a boy yearns to fish like his father or a girl dreams of playing the piano like her mother. Imitation is as much a part of being in God's family as it is in our earthly family.

The Apostle continues with some wise warnings:

> But do not let immorality or any impurity or greed even be named among you, as is proper among saints; and there must be no filthiness and silly talk, or coarse jesting, which are not fitting, but rather giving of thanks. For this you know with certainty, that no immoral or impure person or covetous man, who is an idolater, has an inheritance in the kingdom of Christ and God. Let no one deceive you with empty words, for because of these things the wrath of God comes upon the sons of disobedience. Therefore do not be partakers with them; for you were formerly darkness, but now you are light in the Lord; walk as children of light. (vv. 3–8)

If we claim to be God's sons and daughters, our walk must reflect the light we bear. It would be unfitting for children of light to lurk in dark alleys or wander in shadows. So Paul cautions us:

> Therefore be careful how you walk, not as unwise men, but as wise, making the most of your time, because the days are evil. So then do not be foolish, but understand what the will of the Lord is. (vv. 15–17)

Just what is "the will of the Lord" for us? Paul reveals this often mysterious yet essential issue in an unexpected contrast.

Essential Issue

> Do not get drunk with wine, for that is dissipation, but be filled with the Spirit. (v. 18)

What does a stumbling, weaving drunk have to do with a Christian trying to walk by the Spirit?

Think about the ways alcohol affects people. Before taking a nip, a person may be as timid as a doe hiding in the forest. After a few drinks, though, he or she suddenly turns into a swaggering gorilla. A shy woman may begin singing loudly; a mild-mannered man may start picking fights; a cautious person may take a dare to tiptoe along the ledge of a four-story building. Alcohol transforms people in a negative way, filling them with a cockeyed sort of courage. Paul decries this, calling it dissipation.

The Spirit also transforms people, but in a positive way. Where alcohol obscures good judgment, the Spirit clarifies good judgment. Where alcohol can turn a person

> into an animal, the fullness of the Spirit leads to restrained and rational moral behaviour, transform- ing the Christian into the image of Christ.[1]

The word *fill* can mean filling something to the brim, like a glass of water. But that's not really how the word is used here. The Spirit has already filled us up, or indwelled us fully, the moment we became Christians (see 1 Cor. 3:16). And God never removes the Spirit or commands us to pray for His indwelling.

So, in this context, filling means a continual, moment-by-moment empowering, like wind filling the sails of a boat and push- ing it through the water. Every sailor understands the wind's in- credible power to convert flaccid sails into towering wings that send a yacht skimming, even soaring, across the sea. If the wind holds such force, think of the power within the Creator of the wind!

Amazingly, God has given us a part in this process of being filled with His power. We must open our will to the Spirit, yield control of our lives to Him. Like Jesus in Gethsemane, we need to say, "Not my will, but Thine be done" (see Luke 22:42).

Also, it's important to remember that filling occurs on the in- side. It's not what we do that determines our filling; it's what we choose in our hearts. The Pharisees performed all sorts of righteous deeds, but their hearts were dead to the living God. A ragtag bunch of fishermen disciples, however, gave their hearts to Christ and forever changed the world through the Spirit's power.

Key Hindrance

Such good news for us, yet there's an inescapable problem. We're sinners. When we sin, it's like dropping an anchor that stops us dead in the water. Learning to sail in the Spirit depends on knowing how to handle our sin nature, which Paul explains in Romans 6.

1. John R. W. Stott, *Baptism and Fullness: The Work of the Holy Spirit Today*, 2d ed. (Downers Grove, Ill.: InterVarsity Press, 1979), p. 57.

He begins the chapter by laying some theological groundwork. From God's perspective, when we trust Christ for salvation, we die with Him, are buried with Him, and are raised with Him. The purpose is "so we too might walk in newness of life" (v. 4). Prior to salvation, we walked only along the shadowy paths of our old master, sin. Now we have a new Master and, consequently, a new capacity for righteousness.

But we often still choose to serve our old master. So how do we walk with the new instead of the old?

Three words from verses 5–13 summarize Paul's answer. First, we begin every day *knowing* that God has raised us from the dead and that we are no longer sin's slaves (vv. 6, 9). When that truth moves from our minds to our hearts, we *consider* or reckon it to be true. Not only do we see ourselves in a new light, we believe the implication of what we see—namely, that we're "dead to sin, but alive to God in Christ Jesus" (v. 11). Then our hearts pump that truth to all parts of our bodies as we *present,* or yield, our "members as instruments of righteousness to God" (v. 13). We give God our tongues to let Him control what we say; we give Him our hands to let Him guide what we do; we give Him our eyes to let Him direct what we see.

Presenting ourselves to God leads us full circle to Ephesians 5 and the filling of the Spirit. As J. Dwight Pentecost explains in his book *The Divine Comforter,*

> When the individual says, "I accept God's will for my life, whatever it is, whenever it is revealed, wherever it takes me, once and for all," God's will becomes the determining principle in his life. That act is the presenting or yielding necessary for the filling of the Spirit. There are many of God's children who have never experienced the fullness of the Holy Spirit in their lives, day by day, because they never have come to the place where they are willing to surrender their own wills, their own way, their own wisdom, their own goals, ambitions and desires, to say, "Lord, I am stepping down off the throne of my life, and from this moment on I am acknowledging Your right to my life, to take it and use it as You see fit."[2]

2. J. Dwight Pentecost, *The Divine Comforter: The Person and Work of the Holy Spirit* (1963; reprint, Chicago, Ill.: Moody Press, 1975), p. 161.

That simple prayer epitomizes what it means to walk by the Spirit. Sadly, many of us still crawl through life because we focus on the lure of sin instead of the strength of God. We become more sin-conscious than God-conscious and live scared of sin's power over us. However, by taking the three baby steps of knowing, considering, and presenting, we put our eyes on the Lord. We begin walking in the Spirit's power with confidence.

Practical Results

What will happen in our lives when we start walking? Ephesians 5:19–21 lists five results: we speak "to one another in psalms and hymns and spiritual songs," which implies deeper spiritual relationships with others (v. 19); our hearts sing with grace and our lives become more harmonious (v. 19b); we develop a sense of gratitude to God (v. 20); a spirit of genuine humility takes root in our souls (v. 21a); and we fear the Lord with reverence and awe (v. 21b).

Walking: It's Your Move

Walking by the Spirit is not as complicated as some people make it out to be. It's not something so mystical and profound that only monks, pastors, and professors of theology can understand it. All of us, young or old, can yield control of our lives to the Lord, letting Him direct our steps and fill us with His power.

To conclude our thoughts, let's observe four things about physical walking that are also true of spiritual walking.

- It's a normal part of growth.

- It comes easier the older we get.

- It's a step-by-step action.

- It implies action and movement.

God won't empower us if we sit back in our armchairs analyzing the Christian life but doing nothing. To walk we have to get up and step out in faith. Walking in dependence upon the Lord is our move.

You may feel wobbly and afraid of falling; the first step is always the scariest. But He's sitting right in front of you with video camera in hand, cheering you on. He's prompting you, "C'mon. Come to Me." Once you experience the thrill of walking and all its delights, you'll wonder how you ever got along before.

Tink, tink, tink, tink, tink, tink . . . tink, tink, tink, tink, tink, tink . . . tink, tink, tink, tink, tink, tink, tink . . . _tink, tink._ Recognize the tune?

It's "Chopsticks"—which, spiritually speaking, is about all we can play on God's concert piano apart from His power. Once He fills our fingertips with His Spirit, though . . . da, da, da, _dum._ Beethoven's Fifth Symphony!

If we yield ourselves to the Holy Spirit and rest in His strength, He can do things through us we never imagined possible. Let's explore the Scriptures to discover the kinds of things the Spirit can do. Take a few moments to write down what you find.

Concerning Our Witness

Acts 1:8 _____

Acts 4:8–13 _____

Acts 6:9–10 _____

Acts 8:29–38 _____

Concerning Our Inner Well-Being

Acts 9:31 _____

Acts 13:52 _____

Romans 8:6 _____

Galatians 5:22–23 _____

Ephesians 3:16–19 _____

Concerning Our Ministry

1 Corinthians 2:4–5 _____

1 Corinthians 2:12–13 _____

1 Thessalonians 1:5 _____

Concerning Our Relationship with God

John 16:13–14 _____

Romans 8:26–27 _____

In which of these areas do you most need to rely on the Spirit's power? Why?

_____

_____

_____

Are you willing to yield control of that area to Him? Invite the Spirit to fill you; then get ready to hear the symphony He'll make of your life.

 ## Living Insights

The Holy Spirit is not the only spiritual force controlling us. According to Paul, "the love of Christ controls us" as well (2 Cor. 5:14a). His sacrificial love is like a beautiful melody that overwhelms us and stirs our devotion to Him.

In "The Light Princess," George MacDonald illustrates the power of love's melody through a courageous prince who sacrifices himself to save a bewitched princess. An evil aunt cursed her when she was a child, stealing away her gravity. Under the spell, she became lighter than a puff of dust and would float away if not held down. But in losing her physical weight, she also lost her ability to feel and know the weights of life. Everything, even tragedies, made her laugh. She never cried, and she never smiled.

Her one real pleasure was swimming in the lake near the castle, for when she touched the water, she regained some sense of gravity. And it was there she met a prince, who fell in love with her and swam with her nightly. However, when her wicked aunt learned of her happiness, she cast another spell that slowly drained the lake through an enchanted hole until nothing remained but a few muddy pools. Strangely, as the water ebbed away, so did the princess's spirit.

Seeing her sorrow, the prince determined to restore the lake for his dear princess. A gold plate had been found describing the only means by which the hole could be plugged. It read:

> "The body of a living man should alone stanch the flow. The man must give himself of his own will; and the lake must take his life as it filled. Otherwise the offering would be of no avail. If the nation could

not provide one hero, it was time it should perish."[3]

The prince volunteered to be placed in the hole, asking only that the princess wait in a boat beside him for comfort. He spoke to her of his love, but she responded nonchalantly . . . until the waters began to engulf him.

> The water rose and rose. It touched his chin. It touched his lower lip. It touched between his lips. He shut them hard to keep it out. The princess began to feel strange. It touched his upper lip. He breathed through his nostrils. The princess looked wild. It covered his nostrils. Her eyes looked scared, and shone strange in the moonlight. His head fell back; the water closed over it, and the bubbles of his last breath bubbled up through the water. The princess gave a shriek, and sprang into the lake.[4]

She desperately tugged at the prince, until finally she freed his lifeless body and pushed him into the boat. Rowing to shore, she quickly gave orders to a few servants nearby to carry him to her room.

> The princess was nearly distracted between hope and fear, but she tried on and on, one thing after another, and everything over and over again.
> At last, when they had all but given it up, just as the sun rose, the prince opened his eyes.
> The princess burst into a passion of tears, and *fell* on the floor. There she lay for an hour, and her tears never ceased. All the pent-up crying of her life was spent now. And a rain came on, such as had never been seen in that country. . . . The torrents poured from the mountains like molten gold; and if it had not been for its subterranean outlet, the lake would have overflowed and inundated the country. It was full from shore to shore.[5]

3. George MacDonald, "The Light Princess," in *The Gifts of the Child Christ* (Grand Rapids, Mich.: William B. Eerdmans Publishing Co., 1973), vol. 2, p. 40.

4. MacDonald, "The Light Princess," p. 47.

5. MacDonald, "The Light Princess," p. 48.

The tune of sacrificial love that the prince played on his own life stirred a refrain of love and devotion from deep within the princess's dammed-up heart.

What has been your response to Christ our Prince's sacrifice on your behalf? Do you sometimes feel like the bewitched princess, unmoved by the weight of Christ's love toward you? If so, take this opportunity to unstop the river of emotions in your heart and pour out your devotion, even as the princess poured out her tears. We've provided the following space for you to record your prayer to Him.

_____

_____

_____

_____

_____

Chapter 6

THE DELIGHTS OF CHILDHOOD

Selected Scriptures

When it comes to math, Lenny Ng is a whiz. At age ten, he flew through the math SAT exam, scoring a perfect 800. Then he aced the American High School Math Exam four years in a row—a record performance. In 1992, he calculated his way to a gold medal at the math olympics in Moscow. And when he turned sixteen, the age when most teenagers are struggling to connect the dots in geometry class, he entered Harvard . . . as a sophomore.[1]

Math prodigies like Lenny Ng are rare, but we all have something in common with them. Every one of us entered the world of numbers at the same starting point: $1 + 1 = 2$. Then, after we learned to add, we mastered subtraction, then multiplication, then division. Each stage built upon the previous one, and we had to pass through all of them on our way to graduation.

It's the same way with spiritual development. For example, just as third graders can't comprehend multiplication tables without first understanding addition, we have trouble solving the problems of adolescence without having first survived the trials of childhood. The difference, however, is that we have no achievement tests to measure our maturity; it's our lives that reveal our level of spiritual growth.

One of the most important signs of maturity is our level of self-motivation. When infant believers can obey the Lord, nourish themselves on His Word, talk to Him in prayer, and walk in the Spirit without needing as much hands-on help, they're ready to transition into childhood, the stage we'll consider now.

Analysis of Spiritual Childhood: A Biblical Survey

As we reflect on the stage of spiritual childhood, let's organize our thoughts around three general observations.

---

1. Melinda Beck and Pat Wingert, "The Puzzle of Genius: Where Do Great Minds Come From?" *Newsweek*, June 28, 1993, p. 53.

Children Have Unique Distinctions

It doesn't take a degree in child development to notice that children are different from teenagers and adults, not only in size but also in the way they think. The apostle Paul alludes to these distinctions:

> When I was a child, I used to *speak* as a child, *think* as a child, *reason* as a child; when I became a man, I did away with childish things. (1 Cor. 13:11, emphasis added)

These three verbs Paul chose are in the imperfect tense in Greek, which suggests continuous past action. We can translate them literally, "I kept on speaking . . . thinking . . . reasoning as a child." Children understand only the words and ideas that make up their immediate lives. The sun rises and sets in the sky they see; their teachers live at school; their parents exist solely to care for them. It's not wrong for them to reason in these terms; it's just part of being young.

Thinking that we're helping children put away childish things, we sometimes push them out of their nests of innocence too soon. According to David Elkind in his book *The Hurried Child:*

> Children need time to grow, to learn, and to develop. To treat them differently from adults is not to discriminate against them but rather to recognize their special estate.[2]

In the same way, spiritual children need time to mature in the family of God. "Hurry and grow up" may be all that some young Christians hear from those who are more mature. With an impatient tone of voice or a roll of the eyes, an older believer may unknowingly communicate, "Don't ask such stupid questions" or "Quit making so many messes!" Feeling ashamed of their distinctive needs, many eventually stop asking questions—and stop growing. How much better it is to accept them for who they are and the unique stage of life they're in.

---

2. David Elkind, *The Hurried Child* (Reading, Mass.: Addison-Wesley Publishing Co., 1981), pp. 21–22.

Children Need Parental Accommodations

Because children have special needs, adults have to make certain accommodations for them. Notice Paul's willingness to give of himself to the Corinthians:

> Here for this third time I am ready to come to you, and I will not be a burden to you; *for I do not seek what is yours, but you;* for children are not responsible to save up for their parents, but parents for their children. (2 Cor. 12:14, emphasis added)

When Paul came to them, his desire was not to use or take advantage of them but merely to be with them, to be present for them. Physical as well as spiritual children need this kind of availability; they need to be provided for and protected. Drawing out the comparison, let's list a few specific accommodations children require from their parents.

- Children need time with their parents in order to feel accepted and valuable.

- Children need a secure environment in which their self-esteem can be nurtured.

- Children need healthy communication with their parents. Open conversations become an anvil upon which children hammer out the principles of integrity and moral values.

- Children need a shelter from shameful things. The evils of the world are only too ready to flood young hearts, drowning innocence and trust.

Concerning this last point, it's up to spiritual "parents" to shield young believers until they can handle harsh realities. For instance, carelessly dragging out the skeletons in a church's closet may jeopardize a child's trust in the Lord. It's wiser to wait until their faith has taken root before burdening them with weighty matters.

Children Require Firm Supervision

Our final observation of children is that even as they're gaining independence, they still require firm supervision. The book of Proverbs describes the kind of oversight children require:

> Train up a child in the way he should go,

Even when he is old he will not depart from it.
(22:6)

The rod and reproof give wisdom,
But a child who gets his own way brings shame
    to his mother. (29:15)

Do not withhold discipline from a child;
    if you punish him with the rod, he will not die.
Punish him with the rod
    and save his soul from death.
(23:13–14 NIV; see also 22:15)

As a potter must have a firm, steady hand when shaping the clay, so parents must give strong, consistent guidance to their children. Training is the parents' business—they teach their children the ways of life through moral and relational instruction. A child left to himself, lacking training in knowing good from bad, is on a course to self-destruction. Shaping and disciplining are not optional; they're essential.

As important as discipline is, perhaps even more important is how it is done. In the church, spiritual children are often wrapped in adult skin, so correction requires generous amounts of tact and grace to uphold the person's dignity. Like the potter, whose firm hand gently pressures the whirling clay, we, too, must be mindful of the intensity of our touch.

Delightful Strengths of Spiritual Childhood

Alongside these general observations stand three delightful strengths of children.

Intellectual Teachability and Availability

This first strength shines through the familiar scene of Jesus and the little children. Crowds of people were bringing their children to Him for a blessing, but His protective disciples were trying to keep their Master from being bothered by them. When Jesus saw what was going on, however,

He was indignant and said to them, "Permit the children to come to Me; do not hinder them; for the kingdom of God belongs to such as these. Truly I say to you, whoever does not receive the kingdom

47

of God like a child shall not enter it at all." And
He took them in His arms and began blessing them,
laying His hands upon them. (Mark 10:14–16)

Jesus stresses not only the teachability of children—their openness to receive—but also their touchability as He holds them close
and lays His hands on them. Young Christians, too, with open minds
and wide eyes, receive Jesus and welcome His gentle touch.

Emotional Dependence

This openness and touchability fosters a healthy emotional dependence, a total trust. Imagine the hurt expressions on the children's faces if Jesus had turned them away. By coming to Him, they
had, in a sense, flung themselves emotionally into His arms. Would
He catch them and hold them? Thankfully, yes.

Christians in the childhood stage also exhibit that same kind
of vulnerable trust around more mature believers. Young Christians
may be newly divorced or just out of a cult or have recently endured
some trauma in life. They trust you to lead them into the truth, to
take their hand and bless them.

Spiritual Hunger and Readiness

We discover the third strength in the life of Timothy. Paul
reminded him how, as a child, he learned about spiritual things:

From childhood you have known the sacred writings
which are able to give you the wisdom that leads to
salvation through faith which is in Christ Jesus.
(2 Tim. 3:15)

Like the boy Timothy, children in the Lord are spiritually hungry
and ready to absorb the truths of Scripture. Perhaps this is their
greatest strength.

Examination of Where I Am: Personal Evaluation

Have you ever watched children playing in a pile of leaves?
Squealing and laughing, they jump into the pile, crunch paths
through it, and flop down into it, tossing handfuls of leaves in the
air. Children in the Lord dive into spiritual things with just as much
no-holds-barred energy. With uninhibited faith, they revel in every
new experience with Christ and new truth from His Word. It's
thrilling to witness their joy.

Perhaps you're in this stage of growth right now. Don't hold back your enthusiasm and sense of wonder. It's OK to ask lots of questions, and don't worry if you stumble a little. Your walk with the Lord is fresh and your faith delightfully pure.

But maybe you've moved past this stage. Take time to listen to younger believers, to nurse their scrapes, and to allow them to be children. Supervise them firmly yet lovingly. And let the words of this prayer be yours:

> Father . . .
> Give us patience, perseverance, grace, tact. Round the sharp corners of our lives so that people are not bruised when they're around us. Open our arms to an embrace. Help us to be discerning and know how much to expose to a child's mind, lest we overexpose it and create a confusion in the whole area of shame and moral directives. Help us as adults, while growing, to keep on in the process of telling others of the Savior, being sensitive to them in their needs and accepting them where they are. . . . Make us willing to give up our rights for the good of those who are weak and aren't yet where we are. Graciously help us to be like Your Son, who loved children and who was Himself at one time a child. . . . Amen.[3]

 Living Insights

"Five more minutes," the teacher called out. I remember staring at the gray lump of clay on my desk. *What could I make in five minutes?* The other children's hands were busy putting the finishing touches on their bowls or mugs. My hands were sweating.

"Four minutes."

I rolled the lump between my fingertips, hoping for a shape to spring out like Gumby. But . . . nothing.

"Three minutes."

---

3. Charles R. Swindoll, "The Delights and Dangers of Childhood" (preached at the First Evangelical Free Church of Fullerton, Fullerton, Calif., March 24, 1985).

I could hand in a ball and call it a marble, I thought. *Nah.*
"Two minutes."

Picking up the round clay, I pinched one side. It sort of looked like a nose . . . an idea! Quickly, I took my pencil, poked two eyes, squiggled a mouth under the nose, and broke off two tiny pieces for ears.

"One minute."

Dragging the pencil across the top, I made hair. Then I flattened the bottom so it wouldn't roll. There, finished—a bust of me. Sort of.

Years later, when I was in college, I saw that misshapen figure above the kitchen sink on my mother's plant shelf, where she kept some of her favorite things. "I can't believe you still have that old head," I said. "I think it's wonderful," she said. "You're kidding! The eyes are off center, one side droops—it's funny looking," I said, laughing. "But you made it," she replied gently. "It's you."

Young Christians' first attempts at serving the Lord may resemble my old grade-school ceramics project. Their theology may contain a few cracks; their attempts at giving their testimony may sag a little; their attitudes may lack polish. But it's *them*; it's the best they can give.

How do we respond to their childlike efforts? Do we criticize them? Do we gossip? Or do we treasure their trying and the heart it reflects?

Living Insights STUDY TWO

Have you ever wondered if Jesus wanted to trade in His disciples for a new batch? So often they would forget an important lesson He had just taught them, like the time they were worried about what to eat after Jesus had recently fed five thousand people with only five loaves of bread (see Matt. 16:5–12). Or the time Peter confessed: "Thou art the Christ, the Son of the living God" (v. 16), but soon afterward tried to dissuade Jesus from going to the Cross (vv. 22–23).

Despite the disciples' mistake-prone faith, Jesus stuck with them. He loved them to the end, even though none stood with Him.

Have you ever wondered if Jesus wants to trade you in? Like the disciples, perhaps you have trouble remembering your lessons. You get frustrated at yourself because your walk with God seems more infantile than delightfully childlike. Take a few moments to read the following verses, and jot down Christ's commitment to you as His child.

John 6:37–40 _____

John 10:27–30 _____

Based on the lesson, what childlike qualities are a part of your spiritual life? Write down a few of these that delight your Father so much.

_____

_____

_____

Perhaps the Lord is patient with us now because He knows what we will be like someday. Read 1 John 3:1–2. What encouragement do you find in these verses?

_____

_____

_____

Chapter 7

ADULT TALK ABOUT "CHILDISH THINGS"

Selected Scriptures

Children's eyes are the lamps to their souls. Through them you can see both sides of their nature: the delightful side and the difficult side, the childlike side and the childish side.

Picture a little boy's eyes full of childlike wonder as he gazes at a Christmas tree ribboned with lights. Or the glint of youthful determination as he sets out for a day of Huck Finn adventures. And when a little girl gets the giggles with her friends, how her eyes sparkle with irresistible joy!

But what else do you see in a child's eyes?

There's a shadowy side, isn't there? The temper tantrum's flailing rage or the clutching greed that screams, "This toy is mine!" Dark clouds fill pouting eyes that can flash anger one moment, then spill torrents of tears the next because someone else got a thicker piece of chocolate cake.

Spiritually speaking, we can also be childlike, innocent and trusting; as well as childish, selfish and immature. In the previous chapter, we examined a few delightful childlike qualities. Now let's turn our attention to what Paul called *childish things*.

The Difficult Part: Childishness

> When I was a child, I used to speak as a child, think as a child, reason as a child; when I became a man, I did away with childish things. (1 Cor. 13:11)

Unlike Paul, many of us refuse to let go of childishness as we grow older. On the outside, we have adult bodies, but on the inside, we're still immature children who can slow our own growth through the following four tendencies.

Willfully Defiant

A childish person, first, is willfully defiant. This prideful attitude is as old as sin itself and was the largest stumbling block for the Hebrew people. Notice how the Lord describes them through the pen of Isaiah the prophet:

> "Woe to the rebellious children," declares the Lord,
> "Who execute a plan, but not Mine,
> And make an alliance, but not of My Spirit,
> In order to add sin to sin;
> Who proceed down to Egypt,
> Without consulting Me,
> To take refuge in the safety of Pharaoh,
> And to seek shelter in the shadow of Egypt!"
> (Isa. 30:1–2)

Isaiah continues the indictment, saying they were not willing to listen "To the instruction of the Lord" (v. 9). They wanted the prophets to speak only "pleasant words" and "prophesy illusions" rather than the truth (v. 10). Defiantly, they covered their ears and cried out, "Let us hear no more about the Holy One of Israel" (v. 11b).

Another prophet who exposed the childish Israelites was Jeremiah. Known as the weeping prophet, he must have mourned as he wrote down the Lord's piercing words to them:

> "For My people are foolish,
> They know Me not;
> They are stupid children,
> And they have no understanding.
> They are shrewd to do evil,
> But to do good they do not know." (Jer. 4:22)

In chapter 5, the Lord again calls the people "foolish and senseless" (v. 21). He explains why:

> "'This people has a stubborn and rebellious heart;
> They have turned aside and departed.
> They do not say in their heart,
> "Let us now fear the Lord our God."'"
> (vv. 23–24a; see also Ezek. 2:1–7; 3:1–7)

Forsaking God's path of blessings to follow their own road to destruction was foolish. But that's how defiant children behave, for as Proverbs 22:15 says, "Foolishness is bound up in the heart of a child"—and, we can add, in the heart of a childish adult.

Superficially Committed

The prophet Ezekiel points out another characteristic of childish people: they are superficially committed. Most parents know what this looks like. "Please can we have a puppy?" their children beg. "We'll feed it and play with it every day. Pleeeease!" Finally, they give in. But two weeks later, what happens? The children's interests shift to other things, and Mom and Dad end up taking care of the puppy.

The Israelites' spiritual commitment seemed to be just as short-lived and superficial, as the Lord explained to Ezekiel.

> "Your fellow citizens who talk about you by the walls and in the doorways of the houses, speak to one another, each to his brother, saying, 'Come now, and hear what the message is which comes forth from the Lord.' And they come to you as people come, and sit before you as My people, and hear your words, but they do not do them, for they do the lustful desires expressed by their mouth, and their heart goes after their gain. And behold, you are to them like a sensual song by one who has a beautiful voice and plays well on an instrument; for they hear your words, but they do not practice them." (Ezek. 33:30–32)

Thousands of years have passed since the Lord tailored those words for the children of Israel, but they still fit many churchgoers today, don't they? Many Christians love the songs and the sermons; they talk about the truth, invite others to come listen, even acknowledge that it's from God. But rarely do they put into practice what they hear. They desire to be entertained, not changed.

Willful defiance is one thing, but when we hide that attitude under a sugary glaze of superficial commitment, the results are tragic. We begin leading double lives, worshiping God on Sunday and doing what we please during the week. After all, God is forgiving, isn't He? As long as He doesn't instantly zap us when we break His commandments, we think we can get away with it. But that's childish thinking, and it always leads to heartache.

Overly Impressed

Third, childish people often become overly impressed with popular leaders. To find an example of this characteristic, let's travel through time from ancient Israel to the New Testament church.

Although the Corinthian believers lived in a temperate, lovely Mediterranean port city, storm clouds of bickering often filled their assembly. Perhaps the most immature of all the early Christians, they used to quarrel with one another like children on the playground. Some were shouting, "I am of Paul," and others, "I of Apollos"; others were contending, "I of Cephas," and some, "I of Christ" (see 1 Cor. 1:10–12).

Now, there's nothing wrong with disagreeing with one another and then healing the rift through calm negotiation. But in this case, they were embroiled in such an ugly brouhaha that Paul had to separate the arguers and give them a scolding.

> I, brethren, could not speak to you as to spiritual men, but as to men of flesh, as to babes in Christ. I gave you milk to drink, not solid food; for you were not yet able to receive it. Indeed, even now you are not yet able, for you are still fleshly. For since there is jealousy and strife among you, are you not fleshly, and are you not walking like mere men? (1 Cor. 3:1–4)

In verse 21, he sums up his plea: "So then let no one boast in men." God has provided leaders as our models, but we must be careful not to idolize them (see also 1 John 5:21). It's only natural, particularly when we're young believers, to hang on every word our spiritual parents tell us. The charm that makes them good leaders can draw us to them like magnets. But we must be willing to listen to others; no one person has all the right answers.

Four more reasons reveal the danger of fashioning people into idols.

- *Idols stagnate our knowledge.* In our minds, our mentor's opinions become etched in stone. Whatever position they take on a biblical issue becomes *the* position, and all others are wrong. It is better to balance several opinions and allow the Scripture to guide us to the truth.

- *Idols steal our allegiance.* We can become more loyal to a person than to the Lord. Leaning too heavily on our leader for support, we pray less, we study the Bible for ourselves less, and our ability to trust Christ weakens.

- *Idols strain our balance.* Worshiping people always sets us up for a tumble down the rocky hill of disillusionment. No one can live up to all our expectations or meet our deepest needs except Christ.

- *Idols stunt our growth.* A guarantee for remaining in the spiritual stage of childhood is to become overly impressed with people.

You'll be amazed how you'll grow when you *learn* from people but *worship* the Lord.

Easily Swayed

The fourth characteristic of a childish person is that of being easily swayed. Every day we hear wrenching accounts of children becoming victims because they trusted someone they shouldn't have. Spiritual children also lack discernment, so God provided leaders to nurture young believers. Paul lists them in Ephesians 4:11 as apostles, prophets, evangelists, and pastor-teachers.[1] Verses 12–13 describe their purpose:

> The equipping of the saints for the work of service, to the building up of the body of Christ; until we all attain to the unity of the faith, and of the knowledge of the Son of God, to a mature man.

As a result,

> we are no longer to be children, tossed here and there by waves, and carried about by every wind of doctrine, by the trickery of men, by craftiness in deceitful scheming; but speaking the truth in love, we are to grow up in all aspects into Him, who is the head, even Christ. (vv. 14–15)

Waves of false philosophies crash over us every day through what we see and hear; and young Christians have little scriptural understanding to anchor themselves. They listen to one person and are tossed this way; then to another, and are tossed that way. According to the passage, three different forces blow them off course.

First, "every wind of doctrine" refers to the teaching of religious charlatans. Second, "the trickery of men" is the slick manipulation some people use like loaded dice to sucker naive believers. Third, the "craftiness in deceitful scheming" is the unscrupulous, cunning tactics employed by some to deliberately wash young ones onto the reef. In light of this, commentator William Barclay gives us the following insightful advice:

---

1. The verse reads "pastors and teachers," but many scholars believe the two roles are actually one. A pastor must also be a teacher whose purpose is to feed the body of believers so they can do the work of ministry.

In every Church there are certain members who must be protected. There are those who are like children; they are dominated by a desire for novelty; they are at the mercy of the latest fashion in religion; they are always under the influence of the last person to whom they talked. . . . In every Church there are certain people who have to be guarded against. Paul speaks of the clever trickery of men. . . . There are always those who by clever and ingenious arguments seek to lure people away from their faith. . . .

There is only one way to avoid being blown about by the latest religious fashion, and to avoid being seduced by the specious arguments of clever men, and that is by continual growth into Christ, by living nearer and closer to Him every day.[2]

The Diligent Part: Growing Up beyond Childhood

Let's build upon William Barclay's challenge with three final stones of counsel. First, *we dare not remain childish.* An immature person can wreak havoc in the family of God. So let's not be satisfied with the way things are; let's look for attitudes and habits we can change for the better.

Second, *we must not ignore our responsibility.* Sometimes parents blame themselves for their children who have grown up to be childish adults. But somewhere along the line their children simply refused to mature. No one can grow up for us; it's our responsibility to come to terms with our defiant nature, to stop excusing our superficiality, to guard against idol worshiping, to protect ourselves against false teaching.

Third, *we cannot escape the tension between our nature and our need.* It's a lot less trouble to remain childish. It pleases our fleshly nature, and it feels good when others spoil us at times. But growing up is essential. The church will never reach its potential for effective ministry until we do. Won't you have a heart-to-heart talk with your childish side?

2. William Barclay, *The Letters to the Galatians and Ephesians*, 2d ed., The Daily Study Bible Series (Philadelphia, Pa.: Westminster Press, 1958), pp. 178–79.

One of the most childish adults in the Old Testament is King Saul. Remember when the Philistines were pressing in and he foolishly offered the burnt offering himself instead of waiting for Samuel? Then he tried excusing his mistake, saying to Samuel, "You did not come within the appointed days . . . so I forced myself and offered the burnt offering" (1 Sam. 13:11b, 12b).

Then there was the time he spared the Amalekite king, Agag, and the best of the livestock, even though God had told him to "utterly destroy all that he has, and do not spare him" (15:3a). When Samuel confronted Saul, he put the blame on the people, saying they kept some of the spoil to sacrifice to the Lord. But Samuel replied, "Behold, to obey is better than sacrifice" (v. 22), and,

"Because you have rejected the word of the Lord,
He has also rejected you from being king." (v. 23b)

Saul cried out,

"I have sinned. . . . I feared the people and listened to their voice. Now therefore, please pardon my sin and return with me, that I may worship the Lord." (vv. 24–25)

But Saul only wanted his kingdom back and to save face in front of his officials. Samuel did return with him so he could worship the Lord, but it was just a show (see vv. 30–31).

Can you see some of the characteristics of childishness in Saul? Willful defiance? Superficial commitment? Being overly impressed with people and easily swayed?

Now take a look at your own life for a few moments. Perhaps you've been cutting corners lately, sacrificing but not fully obeying. Maybe it's because of a defiant attitude that has been creeping into your heart. If so, unveil some of those secret thoughts here.

_____

_____

_____

Like Saul, perhaps you realize you've been listening to people more than God. Have you become enamored of someone else's opinions, maybe overly impressed by them so that you're following them rather than God? Name the people who sway your thinking the most. Are they leading you to or away from the Lord?

_____

_____

_____

Finally, evaluate your commitment to the Lord. Is it sincere or a little showy? When you sing or pray, do you focus on the Lord or do thoughts of impressing others enter your mind? In the following space, reaffirm your desire to serve the Lord with a whole heart.

_____

_____

_____

 ## Living Insights STUDY TWO

With a story from her childhood, Anne Ortlund illustrates our childish tendency to go to church to be entertained instead of changed.

> When I was little we used to play church. We'd get the chairs into rows, fight over who'd be preacher, vigorously lead the hymn singing, and generally have a great carnal time.
>
> The aggressive kids naturally wanted to be up front, directing or preaching. The quieter ones were content to sit and be entertained by the up-fronters.
>
> Occasionally we'd get mesmerized by a true sensationalistic crowd-swayer—like the girl who said, "Boo! I'm the Holy Ghost!" But in general, if the up-fronters were pretty good they could hold their audience quite a while. If they weren't so good, eventually the kids would drift off to play something else—like jump rope or jacks.
>
> Now that generation has grown up, but most of

them haven't changed too much. Every Sunday they still play church. They line up in rows for the entertainment. If it's pretty good, their church may grow. If it's not too hot, eventually they'll drift off to play something else—like yachting or wife swapping.

Not often do churchgoers find themselves in the Presence!

But when they do—

All is changed.[3]

True worship is life-changing. Take a few minutes to look up the following verses and write down some of the things people in the Bible did in response to being in the Lord's presence and receiving His commands.

Genesis 35:1–3 _____

Exodus 24:3 _____

2 Chronicles 5:11–14 _____

Nehemiah 8:9–10 _____

The next time you sit down in church for worship, when the pastor prays or the director leads hymns or the choir sings, think to yourself: "I'm not here to be entertained. Lord, change me like You did Your people long ago." Church may never be the same!

3. Anne Ortlund, *Up with Worship: How to Quit Playing Church*, rev. ed. (Ventura, Calif.: Regal Books, 1982), pp. 10–11.

Chapter 8

THREE PROOFS OF GROWTH

Matthew 10:1–10; Acts 4:32–37

A whole inch!" you exclaim to your beaming child as you draw a new mark on the family growth chart. Sooner than you think, your little ones' marks will overtake your own, and your children will have reached their full stature. They'll have grown up physically; but what about spiritually? Do they ever stop climbing the rungs of their spiritual growth chart? Do we?

Unfortunately, spiritual growth is not as automatic as physical growth. While our bodies jump in obedience to glandular commands, our fleshly nature can refuse the Spirit's promptings. We can stop growing.

If the Lord were to measure your life on a spiritual growth chart, where would He mark your height today in comparison to three or four years ago? Are you happily enjoying a spurt, or has your growth stalled recently?

Think for a moment how tall the disciples grew while they were with Jesus. By the time He left for heaven and gave them the Spirit at Pentecost, these rough-and-tumble fishermen were mature enough to parent the newborn church. That's remarkable growth! What stimulated their rapid development? Jesus emphasized to His disciples three important growth principles that appear in Matthew 10. Let's visit the Lord and His men during a private moment of instruction so we can learn and grow too.

Reviewing Three Principles from Jesus' Teaching

Until now, the disciples had just been observers. They had seen Jesus heal the sick, cast out demons, and address the multitudes. As faithful companions, they had followed Him across the hills and through the lush valleys of Galilee; they had traveled from city to city, synagogue to synagogue, and house to house with Him. Now it was time for them to try ministering on their own. So Jesus sent them out with these instructions:

"Do not go in the way of the Gentiles, and do not

enter any city of the Samaritans; but rather go to the lost sheep of the house of Israel." (Matt. 10:5b–6)

Over the past few months, Jesus had kept them together as a team of twelve; now He was breaking the huddle. However, according to Mark 6:7, Jesus didn't send the disciples out alone but in pairs—a fact which leads us to the first principle of spiritual growth.

Regarding Unity

There is strength in staying close together. When soldiers dig fox-holes, they always dig them big enough for two. It's terrifying to go into battle alone, but with a companion, there is strength. Solomon, the wisest man of his day, concurred:

> Two are better than one because they have a good return for their labor. For if either of them falls, the one will lift up his companion. But woe to the one who falls when there is not another to lift him up. Furthermore, if two lie down together they keep warm, but how can one be warm alone? And if one can overpower him who is alone, two can resist him. A cord of three strands is not quickly torn apart. (Eccles. 4:9–12)

Unity was also on Jesus' mind as He prayed passionately for His disciples—and us—just hours before His death:

> "Holy Father, keep them in Thy name, the name which Thou hast given Me, that they may be one, even as We are. . . . I do not ask in behalf of these alone, but for those also who believe in Me through their word; that they may all be one; even as Thou, Father, art in Me, and I in Thee, that they also may be in Us; that the world may believe that Thou didst send Me. And the glory which Thou hast given Me I have given to them; that they may be one, just as We are one; I in them, and Thou in Me, that they may be perfected in unity, that the world may know that Thou didst send Me, and didst love them, even as Thou didst love Me." (John 17:11b, 20–23)

"That they may be perfected *into a unit*" was His request, literally. Jesus desires that we become a close-knit family. Nothing has

62

damaged His message more than the breakdown of this unit. Church splits, splinter groups, and scandals isolate people, resulting in cynicism and bitterness. "Stay together," Christ pleads. There's strength, and ultimately growth, in unity.

Regarding Authority

The second principle relates to the authority Jesus gave the disciples before sending them out—

> authority over unclean spirits, to cast them out, and to heal every kind of disease and every kind of sickness. (Matt. 10:1b)

The Greek word for "authority" is *exousia*, which means *"liberty or power to act."*[1] It's the power of one whose will or command must be obeyed, like the power of a police officer who stops hundreds of cars by simply raising a hand. So the disciples now had power to bring disease, demons, and even death to a screeching halt.

The principle of growth is this: *there is power in doing God's work.* Power from God's very throne. Are you doing His work? Do it in Christ's power and authority. Declare His message confidently, not because of who you are but because of who He is.

Regarding Generosity

The third principle is this: *there is freedom in giving without restraint.* Jesus instructed His disciples,

> "Freely you received, freely give. Do not acquire gold, or silver, or copper for your money belts, or a bag for your journey, or even two tunics, or sandals, or a staff; for the worker is worthy of his support." (vv. 8b–10)

They may only have had the sky for their ceiling and the earth for their bed, but they were rich with Jesus' presence and authority. So, having bountifully received, they were to give to others. Their gospel message and divine power were not goods to be sold but gifts to be given away.[2]

1. G. Abbott-Smith, *A Manual Greek Lexicon of the New Testament*, 3d ed. (Edinburgh, Scotland: T. and T. Clark, 1937), p. 161.

2. The apostle Paul modeled a generous spirit. He didn't charge people to hear him teach (1 Cor. 9:18). And Peter instructed elders to "shepherd the flock of God among you . . . not for sordid gain, but with eagerness" (1 Pet. 5:2).

In addition, Jesus wanted them to travel light. With no entangling worries about money or possessions, they were to experience the true freedom of trusting God alone. We, too, can experience that by not clinging to what God has given us. Freely you received, so freely give. And freely you will live.

Modeling Those Principles in the Early Church

Well, the disciples went out as Jesus instructed them. They healed the sick, proclaimed the gospel, and, as a result, they grew (see Mark 6:12–13). Later, when Jesus left them to return to heaven, the Holy Spirit filled them with new authority and power on the Day of Pentecost. Soon thousands in Jerusalem were born again because of their gospel message.

As leaders of the early church, the disciples were faced with the monumental task of helping these spiritual babies grow. On what principles of growth do you think they nurtured them? The very ones they had learned from Jesus. Let's take a look at Acts 4 to find out how the next generation of believers lived out these principles.

Unity in Action

> And the congregation of those who believed were of one heart and soul; and not one of them claimed that anything belonging to him was his own; but all things were common property to them. (v. 32)

The early believers didn't just talk about unity, they lived it. They believed the same gospel, they related together in harmony, and they shared what they owned. If someone was hungry or without clothing, they willingly pooled their resources to help. In very practical ways, Jesus' prayer for unity was being answered.

So vital is this sense of unity to the life of the church that, years later, Paul entreated Christ's followers:

> Walk in a manner worthy of the calling with which you have been called, with all humility and gentleness, with patience, showing forbearance to one another in love, being diligent to preserve the unity of the Spirit in the bond of peace. (Eph. 4:1b–3)

The work of unity is a task for us all. It will take effort and maturity to be peacekeepers rather than peace killers. We must be willing to relinquish some of our rights, to make wise compromises, and to be accountable to one another.

Isolating ourselves from each other is tempting, particularly in our modern, I-leave-you-alone-you-leave-me-alone culture. But Christ knows that His church is healthiest when its members are "one heart and soul." If you've stopped growing because you've drifted away from other believers, won't you take some steps toward putting unity into action in your life soon?

Authority on Display

The early church also displayed the second principle: authority.

> And with great power the apostles were giving witness to the resurrection of the Lord Jesus, and abundant grace was upon them all. (Acts 4:33)

God's grace filled the church and became a bridge of respect and trust between the people and the leaders, who were proclaiming Christ's message with authority and power. The church was made up of what writer Howard Snyder calls Kingdom people rather than Church people.

> Church people think about how to get people into the church; Kingdom people think about how to get the church into the world. Church people worry that the world might change the church; Kingdom people work to see the church change the world.[3]

In order to produce Kingdom people today, Christian leaders should view the church as a place for believers to huddle, like players on a football team, to receive biblical instruction and a moment of rest. The real game occurs during the week, as the team members live out their beliefs and proclaim Jesus Christ in the world.

Generosity Applied and Exemplified

The early Christians applied Jesus' generosity principle in an inspiring way.

> For there was not a needy person among them, for all who were owners of land or houses would sell them and bring the proceeds of the sales, and lay

---

3. Howard A. Snyder, *Liberating the Church* (Downers Grove, Ill.: Inter-Varsity Press, 1983), p. 11.

them at the apostles' feet; and they would be distributed to each, as any had need.

And Joseph, a Levite of Cyprian birth, who was also called Barnabas by the apostles (which translated means, Son of Encouragement), and who owned a tract of land, sold it and brought the money and laid it at the apostles' feet. (Acts 4:34–37)

This was not an early form of communism. No one forced the people to sell their goods and distribute the money evenly among everyone. Rather, their irrepressible devotion to the Lord motivated them to give. Commentator Everett Harrison insightfully observes,

> The Church, caught up in the enthusiasm of sacrificial giving, was content to leave the future with God.[4]

In God We Trust may not have been printed on their money, but it was certainly inscribed in their actions. A generous attitude naturally follows when Christ is Lord in a person's life.

Putting Those Principles into Practice Today

Unity. Authority. Generosity. Jesus gave these principles of growth to the disciples, who passed them on to the early Christians, who now offer them to you. Are you hoping for a spiritual growth spurt in your life? Based on these truths, here are a few words of healthy advice. Stay close to people, remember who's really Lord in your life, and hold your treasure loosely. Do these things, and you'll be amazed how tall you'll grow in a short period of time. More than an inch!

 Living Insights STUDY ONE

Perhaps God expressed the most telling truth about the human race when He observed, "It is not good for the man to be alone" (Gen. 2:18a). Isolation wasn't good for Adam, and neither is it good for us. Yet, according to Charles Swindoll, togetherness doesn't come naturally.

---

4. Everett F. Harrison, *Acts: The Expanding Church* (Chicago, Ill.: Moody Press, 1975), p. 90.

We are independent cogs in complex corporate structures. We wear headsets as we jog or do our lawns or walk to class or eat in cafeterias. Our watchword is "privacy"; our commitments are short-term. Our world is fast adopting the unwritten regulation so often observed in elevators, "Absolutely no eye contact, talking, smiling, or relating without written permission from the management." The Lone Ranger, once a fantasy hero, is now our model, mask and all.[5]

We may don the Lone Ranger's mask for many reasons: insecurity, fear of being hurt, prejudice. Do you mask yourself from others? In what ways? Can you pinpoint some reasons?

_____

_____

_____

_____

Isolating ourselves is one reason our churches tend to lack unity. To bring about the oneness for which Jesus prayed, let's begin with our closest circle within the church: our family. How can you unmask yourself more in your relationship with your parents? Spouse? Children? Brothers or sisters?

_____

_____

_____

_____

Accomplishing some of these goals is enough of an assignment for now. But as you begin closing your family circle, consider ways to tighten your spiritual family circle at church. Some of the honest communication and genuineness you develop in your family could spill over into other relationships. When one Lone Ranger takes off his or her mask, other Lone Rangers are sure to follow.

5. Charles R. Swindoll, *Strengthening Your Grip* (Dallas, Tex.: Word Publishing, 1982), p. 29.

Quoting Jesus' statement, "Freely you received, freely give," is much easier than living it. Let's focus on ways to put His words into practice.

First, think of all the things you receive free of charge. Friends may give you their time and wise counsel. You probably receive gifts on birthdays or holidays or at showers. A church member may bring over a meal when you're sick. Neighbors may offer the use of their car when yours is in the shop. The greatest gift of all, of course, is from Christ, who gives you hope and salvation.

Because you've received so much, what can you freely give? Money may initially come to mind. What are some other things? A listening ear for a friend. Baby-sitting for a young couple. A day of rest for your spouse. Try listing some things yourself.

_____   _____

_____   _____

_____   _____

Now wrap up one of these ideas and give it this week with a grateful heart for all you've received.

Chapter 9

ADOLESCENTS IN ADULT BODIES

Selected Scriptures

"I want always to be a little boy and to have fun," grins Peter Pan. Then with one grand leap, he stretches out his arms and flies into the night toward the brightest star and Never Never Land.

As children, millions of us followed Peter's pixie-dust trail to his land of rollicking adventures and returned with hearts full of fantasies. As grown-ups, we never lose our admiration for Peter—the boy eternal. With a magical whirl, he always manages to evade the hook of adulthood. Nothing, not even the ever-ticking, clock-swallowing crocodile, spoils his fun or his freedom.

A little bit of Peter Pan resides in all of us. He's our spirit of youth who likes to crow from time to time. Problems arise, however, when we *always* want to live like the Pan. Psychologist Dan Kiley, in his book *The Peter Pan Syndrome*, describes people with this attitude:

> They don't want anything to do with school, work, or anything else that smacks of adulthood. Their desire is to do whatever they must to remain just what they are: little children who won't grow up.[1]

Kiley actually sees Peter Pan as an illustration of a confused adolescent.

> For all his gaiety, he was a deeply troubled boy . . . caught in the abyss between the man he didn't want to become and the boy he could no longer be.[2]

Spiritually, we can get stuck in that same abyss, becoming adolescents in adult bodies. Our playful desire to never grow up can backfire, affecting not just us but those we love. Let's look at a few characteristics of believers who are lost in the Peter Pan syndrome.

---

1. Dan Kiley, *The Peter Pan Syndrome: Men Who Have Never Grown Up* (New York, N.Y.: Dodd, Mead and Co., 1983), p. 24.

2. Kiley, *The Peter Pan Syndrome*, p. 23.

Undeniable Characteristics of Adolescence

The first earmark of adolescent believers is *instability when the going gets rough.* Instead of "a long obedience in the same direction," as one writer described the Christian walk, they obey the Lord with short bursts in different directions—especially when the trail is rocky and steep.

Another trait is *irresponsibility when the world gets appealing.* A few light breezes of temptation they can handle. But they break easily in a stiff wind of worldly pressure and quickly toss aside their commitments to the Lord and their families.

Finally, they display *insensitivity when the will gets challenged.* When anyone disagrees with them, they usually dig in their heels and insist on having their own way. Plugging their ears, they refuse to listen to the other side or receive wise counsel. "My mind is made up, so don't confuse me with the facts" is their adolescent attitude.

First-Century Examples of Adolescent Adults

In the New Testament, three people in particular put flesh and blood on these characteristics. Illustrating the first trait, *instability,* is John Mark—the first missionary dropout.

John Mark, Who Walked Away

Young John Mark was a rising star on the early church's glowing horizon.[3] Barnabas and Saul saw so much potential in him that they took him from Jerusalem, where believers there used to gather in his mother's house (see Acts 12:12), and brought him to Antioch—the new center for world outreach (v. 25). With great anticipation, John Mark traveled alongside his mentors, perhaps reveling in his chance to rub shoulders with them and idealistically dreaming of future ministries in faraway places.

After they arrived in Antioch, the Holy Spirit set apart Barnabas and Saul to be the early church's first missionaries, so "they went down to Seleucia and from there they sailed to Cyprus" (13:4). But not without John Mark, whom they selected "as their helper" (v. 5b).

---

3. This section has been adapted from "When the Going Gets Rough," from the study guide *The Growth of an Expanding Mission: A Study of Acts 10:1–18:18,* coauthored by Bryce Klabunde, from the Bible-teaching ministry of Charles R. Swindoll (Anaheim, Calif.: Insight for Living, 1992), pp. 68–76.

His youthful idealism must have flourished on the beautiful island of Cyprus. According to William Barclay, the island

> was sometimes called Makaria, which means the Happy Isle, because it was held that its climate was so perfect and its resources so varied that a man might find everything necessary for a happy life within its bounds.[4]

Cyprus was the Hawaii of the first century—not a bad place to visit on a missions trip! Certainly, its charisma must have impressed John Mark when the men disembarked at Salamis, the largest city on the island. Once there, "They began to proclaim the word of God in the synagogues of the Jews" (v. 5). Eventually, they worked their way "through the whole island" (v. 6a), until they reached Paphos, the capital city on the island's opposite side. Here John Mark watched Saul, now called Paul, square off with a demonic magician named Elymas, who

> was opposing them, seeking to turn the proconsul [Sergius Paulus] away from the faith. (v. 8b)

John Mark's heart must have pounded as Paul and the magician clashed. By the time it was over, though, the Lord had blinded Elymas and the proconsul had believed the gospel (see vv. 9–12). It was a spectacular demonstration of God's power; but the episode appears to have shaken John Mark, for the very next verse says,

> Paul and his companions put out to sea from Paphos and came to Perga in Pamphylia; and John left them and returned to Jerusalem. (v. 13)

Why did John Mark leave for home? Although Scripture doesn't spell out the details, we do know Paul called his return to Jerusalem a desertion and refused to take him on subsequent missionary journeys (see 15:36–38). What happened?

We can piece together one theory. Disease was rampant in the coastal area around Perga, and some suggest that Paul contracted malaria there. William Barclay describes the headaches associated with this disease "like a red-hot bar thrust through the forehead."[5]

---

4. William Barclay, *The Acts of the Apostles*, rev. ed., The Daily Study Bible Series (Philadelphia, Pa.: Westminster Press, 1976), pp. 99–100.

5. Barclay, *The Acts of the Apostles*, p. 102.

The only relief for Paul was to escape to the cooler inland mountain regions. And the only route was a rugged road notorious for danger from thieves.

Apparently, that was enough for John Mark. Their experience on Cyprus had deflated him, but when sudden disease and danger met them in Perga, any remaining courage fell to pieces. With his idealism shattered, adolescent John Mark was too unstable to handle the hard times.

Demas, Who Loved the World

Demas is an example of the second characteristic of spiritual adolescence, *irresponsibility*. His name appears only three times in the New Testament, but those passing references provide us a good thumbnail sketch of this man.

Paul first mentions him alongside his longtime friend, Luke, as one of several people who send greetings to the believers in Colossae (see Col. 4:14). And in his letter to Philemon, he includes him with a group of people he calls his "fellow workers" (v. 24). Apparently, Demas was one of Paul's traveling companions who helped him in his itinerant ministry. He was a fellow soldier in the field, a brother in Christ, a friend.

But in his final letter before his execution in Rome, aging Paul writes to Timothy from a dimly lit prison cell:

> Make every effort to come to me soon; for Demas, having loved this present world, has deserted me and gone to Thessalonica; Crescens has gone to Galatia, Titus to Dalmatia. Only Luke is with me. Pick up Mark and bring him with you, for he is useful to me for service. (2 Tim. 4:9–11)

Demas and John Mark have switched places, haven't they? John Mark is now the useful one, and Demas is the deserter.[6] For years, Demas has been faithful both to the Lord and to Paul. But now, like a husband who has abandoned his wife for another woman,

---

6. The Greek word for *desert, egkataleipō,* means "'to abandon . . . leave in straits, leave helpless, leave in the lurch, let one down.' This tells us that Demas had not only left Paul so far as fellowship was concerned, but he had left him in the lurch also, so far as the work of the gospel was concerned. . . . Paul was in prison, his freedom of action curtailed. Here was one who had his liberty, and who deserted the Christian work for the world." Kenneth S. Wuest, *Wuest's Word Studies from the Greek New Testament* (Fincastle, Va.: Scripture Truth Book Co., 1966), vol. 2, p. 164.

Demas has run away with his beguiling mistress, the world.

Paul's path included prison, torture, and death. In contrast, Rome offered Demas

> the magnificent halls of the Caesars, the gorgeous homes of the rich and the glitter of a world of music, venal loves, jest and wine. Such a gay world cast its glamor over Demas, and he yielded to its charms.[7]

He probably didn't fall in love with the world overnight; it was a slow seduction. His decision began with a thought, perhaps while passing a tavern or pagan temple: *Look at those people having fun.* Worldly visions and melodies began lingering in his mind, until finally he secretly succumbed to the temptation. Eventually, he tossed aside his responsibilities like shackles and ran headlong into the charmer's lair.

Has the world's luring siren song been caressing your ears? Before following its sweet, intoxicating airs, remember the tragic story of Demas and the heartache of those who loved him.

Diotrephes, Who Wanted His Way

The third characteristic of spiritual adolescence, *insensitivity,* is illustrated by Diotrephes. Although he's mentioned only once in Scripture, the brief reference in John's third epistle speaks volumes about this type of person.

> I wrote something to the church; but Diotrephes, who loves to be first among them, does not accept what we say. For this reason, if I come, I will call attention to his deeds which he does, unjustly accusing us with wicked words; and not satisfied with this, neither does he himself receive the brethren, and he forbids those who desire to do so, and puts them out of the church. (3 John 9–10)

Adolescent Christians who are like Diotrephes love to be first. They want to be in charge, to have their way, to hold a position of influence where they can make things happen. They also struggle with those in authority. Diotrephes, for example, wouldn't accept

7. Herbert Lockyer, *All the Men of the Bible* (Grand Rapids, Mich.: Zondervan Publishing House, 1958), pp. 91–92.

what John had to say to him. Notice, too, Diotrephes' underhanded tactics. He unjustly accused an apostle, became resistant to new people coming into the church, and excommunicated anyone who disagreed with him. He had become what is sometimes called a "church boss."

Certainly, adolescent Christians like Diotrephes don't set out to destroy the church. Many of them sincerely love the Lord and are the church's most dedicated members. But as pastors who deal with them know, they can easily become what one writer has labeled "well-intentioned dragons."

Of course, not every person who disagrees with you is a "dragon." But watch out for people who frequently breathe fiery criticisms and claw to get their way. Their insensitivity always gives them away as adolescents in adult bodies.

Ways to Guard against "Permanent Adolescence"

How can we grow out of the Peter Pan syndrome and be more stable when the going gets rough, more responsible when the world gets appealing, and more humble when the will gets challenged?

First, *when wrestling with restlessness, realize the benefits of faithfulness.* When you're tempted to find greener, more peaceful pastures during a rough time, think instead of the long-range benefits faithfulness will produce. Second, *when allured by irresponsibility, think of the consequences of carnality.* Stop and visualize the wake of devastation your sin will cause to your spouse, your family, your church . . . yourself. Is it really worth it? Third, *when tempted to manipulate and dominate, remember the lordship of Christ.* Who's ultimately in charge? We don't have to push our way if we're willing to trust our true Master.

Adolescence is a passage through which all of us must travel. The good news is that it's not a dead end. Thankfully, Christ's light at the end of the tunnel is always shining to show us the way through.

 Living Insights STUDY ONE

The gossip mill must have been buzzing when the news about John Mark, Demas, and Diotrephes grapevined through the early church.

"Can you believe John Mark turned tail for home at the first sign of real trouble?"

"I told his mother he wouldn't make it, but did she listen to me?"
"And Demas . . . shocking, simply shocking!"
"By the way, who put that Diotrephes in charge? He's a tyrant."
"Just like his father. I'm tellin' you, he's just like his father."

It's tempting to join the circle and point out all the specks in their eyes, isn't it? But before pulling up a chair and getting too comfortable, let's look for a few logs in our own.

- Have you ever run away from a problem or an overwhelming task?

- Have you ever chucked a responsibility to pursue the world's pleasures and left someone else in the lurch?

- Have you ever responded defensively to someone else's challenging counsel and determined to do it your way no matter what?

All of us have adolescent tendencies. To help curb them, follow the advice given in the last part of the lesson. If you tend to be restless, sometimes abandoning difficult tasks, write down the benefits of sticking with it—benefits to the Lord, to others, and to yourself. Try to refer to a specific trying responsibility in your work or ministry or family as an example.

_____   _____

_____   _____

What worldly vice lures you the most? Write down the consequences of succumbing to that temptation—affecting the Lord, others, and yourself.

_____   _____

_____   _____

Do you tend to dominate? If so, who do you most often manipulate to get your way? How will remembering that Christ is in charge help you humble yourself and lead with a kinder heart?

_____   _____

_____   _____

_____   _____

Now tuck the answers to these questions in your mind to read to your adolescent side whenever it starts poking around uninvited.

Living Insights

How do we help an adolescent believer grow up? Barnabas illustrates the first strategy. Read Acts 15:36–39 and contrast the approaches Paul and Barnabas took with John Mark.

Paul's Approach   Barnabas' Approach

_____   _____

_____   _____

Barnabas' name means "Son of Encouragement" (4:36). In what ways can you take the encouragement approach with a John Mark-type adolescent in your life?

_____

_____

_____

The apostle John models another strategy, confrontation. According to 3 John 9, how did he confront Diotrephes initially? In verse 10, what did he plan to do next?

_____

_____

Although John's letter is gentle and loving, he is firm with Diotrephes, stating the facts clearly. Is this an appropriate way to handle a Diotrephes in your life? How would you implement it?

_____

_____

_____

Dealing with a Demas is more difficult. Because Demas had fled to Thessalonica, perhaps pursuing his worldly loves, the grieving

76

Apostle could only pray for Demas and allow him to reap the bitter wind. Do you know a Demas? In the space provided, express your prayer for this person, placing him or her once again in the hands of God.

_____

_____

_____

_____

_____

_____

Chapter 10

WHEN PETER PAN COMES TO CHURCH

1 Corinthians 1:4–11; 3:1–4; 5:1–2; 8:1–13

The open seas, the salt air, the rushing wind in the sails—ah, that's for me! Honey, I'm going to buy a yacht!" the beaming middle-aged man announced. Silently, his patient wife wondered if his moorings had finally come loose; aloud, she suggested, "But dear, you've never been sailing in your life."

"Nonsense! Why, when I was in high school, Harry and I used to take the *Lucky Lu* out all the time!"

"Yes, but that boat had only one sail, and the pond wasn't more than two hundred yards across, and Harry did all the work . . ."

"Oh, now, honey, size means nothing; the basic principles are all the same. With a little practice, everything will come back to me in no time. You'll see. Trust me."

After several weeks of study and practice, the sea dog invited his wife to join him for a sail. Gingerly stepping aboard, she found a seat near a life preserver and readied herself for the ride. "Now don't you worry," he confidently reassured her, "I've practiced enough in this harbor to know where every rock and sandbar is. Everything will be just fi—" C-R-U-N-C-H! A huge, submerged rock made the hull's acquaintance, from stem to stern.

"There," the mid-life mariner sheepishly grinned, "that's one of them now!"

Knowledge without the experience of wisdom can indeed be a rocky thing. In many ways, that combination characterizes the stage of adolescence—both physical and spiritual. An adolescent may love the fun of sailing through life but lack the wisdom of knowing where the rocks are. In this chapter, let's map out a few of the rough spots hidden beneath the surface of spiritual adolescence, remembering that this stage isn't limited to a certain age or even to individuals. It can mark entire churches . . . like the Peter Pan church that alighted in Corinth.

Biblical Example: A Local Church

In many ways, the Corinthian church had a lot going for it.

Corinth itself was a bustling city that controlled two harbors on either side of a narrow isthmus, making it a center of commerce and a melting pot of freewheeling lifestyles. Ministry opportunities abounded in this trendsetting town, for it was truly a vanity fair filled with thousands of people in paganism's dark grip.

To meet the challenges of this culture, God had supplied the believers in this church with everything they needed to shine brightly for Him. He gave them Paul, who established them in the gospel, and the eloquent Apollos, who built them up on Paul's foundation. So when Paul wrote to them a few years later, he reminded them of their spiritual wealth and thanked God for how He had enriched them

> in all speech and all knowledge, even as the testimony concerning Christ was confirmed in you, so that you are not lacking in any gift. (1 Cor. 1:5b–7a)

Sitting at the feet of some of the finest Christian teachers in the world, these people knew the truth. They had experienced the Spirit's power. Yet for all their knowledge and spiritual gifts, their lack of wisdom made God's household in Corinth as messy as an adolescent's bedroom.

There were things scattered all around. There were things they didn't pick up. There were things they didn't take care of. There were things they didn't clean up. Some were relational, others were theological—most were personal. Let's look at four of the problems this church encountered because of its adolescent attitude.

Great Anxiety

Their first blockade resulted from battles that continually raged in the church, which Paul addressed frankly in verses 10–11.

> Now I exhort you, brethren, by the name of our Lord Jesus Christ, that you all agree, and there be no divisions among you, but you be made complete in the same mind and in the same judgment. For I have been informed concerning you, my brethren, by Chloe's people, that there are quarrels among you. (see also 11:18–19)

Because of the constant contention, an air of great anxiety filled the congregation. Some were waving Paul's words around like banners, while others were marshaling themselves around Apollos, others Cephas (Peter), and a final group was lambasting all teaching except Christ's (v. 12). No one really knew which way to go, and their anxious infighting was fast turning the church into a bloodied battlefield of wounded spirits.

Why was the church behaving this way? They were caught in the Peter Pan syndrome. Many people living in an extended adolescence suffer from anxiety, and author Dan Kiley suggests three reasons why. First, noting that a majority of real-life Peter Pans are firstborns, he has observed that they've struggled with their parents' too-high expectations. Churches, too—especially when they're large and well-known—can be so burdened by others' unrealistic expectations that they lose who they really are; their identity is quashed.

Second, Peter Pans are given to extremes: in moods, perceptions, and decisions. So it is with churches also. They can be extreme in edicts, productions, and positions.

And last, they pretend never to be at fault. "I'm sorry" is not a part of their vocabulary.[1] Churches can become so smug that they either don't admit to faults . . . or they get to the point where they can't even see them.

Personal Immaturity

Another problem waiting beneath the surface in the Corinthian church was the personal immaturity of its members.

> I, brethren, could not speak to you as to spiritual men, but as to men of flesh, as to babes in Christ. I gave you milk to drink, not solid food; for you were not yet able to receive it. Indeed, *even now you are not yet able*, for you are still fleshly. For since there is jealousy and strife among you, are you not fleshly, and are you not walking like mere men? (3:1–3, emphasis added)

When they were new believers, Paul prepared and spoon-fed God's Word to them. But by now they should have been fixing their own meals and taking responsibility for their own growth.

What does spiritual responsibility look like? Scanning the whole of Scripture, we can say that a mature person

---

1. See Dan Kiley, *The Peter Pan Syndrome: Men Who Have Never Grown Up* (New York, N.Y.: Dodd, Mead and Co., 1983), pp. 85–86.

possesses self-discipline
respects authority
stays true to commitments
bears a fair share of the load
is willingly accountable to others
resists extreme independence
serves others unselfishly
maintains moral purity and ethical integrity

The Corinthian church cast off these attributes, particularly the final one—which set them drifting toward the next jagged rock.

Overt Immorality

Nearly sinking the Corinthian church was their problem of overt immorality. Paul wrote with a rebuking pen:

> It is actually reported that there is immorality among you, and immorality of such a kind as does not exist even among the Gentiles, that someone has his father's wife. And you have become arrogant, and have not mourned instead, in order that the one who had done this deed might be removed from your midst. (5:1–2)

We can hardly imagine such immorality going unchecked, yet, apparently, this man was openly living with his "father's wife," probably his stepmother, and no one in the church batted an eye. The congregation should have been calling on God for forgiveness and confronting the man directly. Instead, the people nonchalantly overlooked the sin.

Toleration of sexual immorality is one of the most obvious signs of adolescent congregations. They don't feel comfortable talking about the problem, or they simply find ways to rationalize the sinful behavior. It's an area in which we must grow up, however. We must not wink at promiscuity. Let's call it what it is. Sin. Not unpardonable, but sin nonetheless.[2]

Unrestrained Liberty

Finally, the Corinthian church had run aground because of

---

2. Scripture defines immorality as any sexual intimacy outside of marriage, including sex before marriage, adulterous affairs after marriage, incest, and homosexuality.

unrestrained liberty. Case in point: some believers were publicly eating the meat of animals that had been sacrificed to idols in the local temple—even though that practice caused other believers to stumble. This was as taboo to them as seeing certain movies or having a glass of wine is to some in our day. On one hand, of course, they were free to eat as they liked. Christ never forbade Christians to eat sacrificial meat; and besides, as Paul said,

> We know that there is no such thing as an idol in the world, and that there is no God but one. (8:4b)

The problem was that

> not all men have this knowledge; but some, being accustomed to the idol until now, eat food as if it were sacrificed to an idol; and their conscience being weak is defiled. (v. 7)

These weaker Christians might have tried eating sacrificial meat against their conscience, ruining their faith (see vv. 10–12). So Paul advised the church,

> take care lest this liberty of yours somehow become a stumbling block to the weak. (v. 9)

Modeling a more mature attitude, Paul said he would never eat meat again if that's what it took to protect his fellow Christian from stumbling (v. 13). But adolescent believers exclaim, "Wait a minute! We have our rights. Pass the prime rib!" They have knowledge, but lack wisdom . . . and love.

Concern for others is a guiding principle in a mature congregation. These believers say, "My rights aren't as important as your welfare. I think I'll pass on the prime rib, thank you."

Practical Advice: A Personal Analysis

In this chapter, we've been talking mostly about churches. As we conclude, let's bring this subject closer to home. Do you keep bumping into some of these submerged rocks? Are you trying to sail through life in the SS *Peter Pan?* If so, take some soundings of your heart with these questions:

What am I gaining by remaining immature?
Why am I refusing to model purity?

Who am I hurting by going to extremes in my liberty?
When am I going to come to terms with growing up?

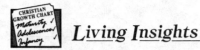 *Living Insights*

Did you skim through those questions too quickly? Let's go back and linger over them for a few minutes.

How well are you handling the responsibilities of adulthood? They can be burdensome, can't they? Sometimes life's pressures can fall on us like a wall of bricks, and it's natural to run for cover and long for the sheltered days of childhood. That's OK. Responsible people aren't always in control and on top of things. But something's not right when we refuse to carry a normal, everyday armload of responsibilities. When that happens, we find ourselves breaking promises, sloughing off our share of work, bucking authority, shutting down relationships . . . in a word, we become adolescents.

Do you see any adolescent attitudes showing up in your life? If so, what types of situations most often usher them in?

_____

_____

_____

Certainly, immature behavior is satisfying, but only for a while. In the long run, what do you gain from remaining immature in a certain area? What do you lose?

_____

_____

_____

Our flight toward freedom from responsibilities often leads us into immorality. If you struggle with sexual sin, can you trace the causes back to an adolescent attitude?

_____

_____

Immature people want their liberty, even at someone else's expense. Do you sometimes demand your rights without considering other people's feelings? Who are you hurting? Do you need to ask their forgiveness?

_____

_____

The last question for you to ask yourself is simply, "When am I going to come to terms with growing up?" Looking in the mirror is the beginning of change—but it is only the beginning. Here are three more steps you can follow toward maturity: first, make up your mind you want to change; second, draw strength from the Holy Spirit by yielding control of these areas to Him (Eph. 5:15–18); and third, tell another Christian about your struggles, asking him or her to pray for you and hold you accountable. Won't you take those steps today?

 Living Insights   STUDY TWO

Have you ever wondered how Noah kept all the animals on the ark from devouring one another? After a few weeks of floating around together, the chickens must have looked mighty tasty to the foxes. And the tigers must have licked their lips hungrily watching a deer stroll by.

But Noah's task was easy compared to a pastor's job of getting the lions and the lambs in the church to lie down together. One church member likes hymns, another likes praise songs; one likes pews, the other likes chairs; one wants the church to hire a youth pastor, the other a children's director. Quarrels, cliques, and controversies. How do we live together without gobbling each other up?

Our Lord gave us the answer when He issued the church's Magna Carta of getting along:

> "This is My commandment, that you love one another, just as I have loved you." (John 15:12)

And Peter wrote, "Above all"—above all the prayer meetings and potlucks and Christmas plays—

> Above all, keep fervent in your love for one another,

because love covers a multitude of sins. (1 Pet. 4:8)

Has a church member committed any "sins" against you? Have you wanted to bite back with criticism? If so, write down this person's name and, in the space provided, a few practical things you can do for this person to show them Christ's love. Cover their offenses with love, and let Christ curb your appetite for revenge.

_____

_____

_____

_____

Chapter 11

WHAT'S *RIGHT* ABOUT ADOLESCENCE?
Selected Scriptures

The stage of adolescence resembles a house on moving day: it's a mess, but it's a temporary one.

Physically, a teenager's life is spent in transit, going somewhere else to be unpacked. And to complicate the move, the hormones are kicking out the slats of the moving crates.

Spiritually, adolescence is equally an uphill road to adulthood— an adventure in moving!

But in spite of the problems in packing and the chuckholes along the way, there are some good things about this stage of spiritual growth. And in this study we want to answer the question "What's *right* about adolescence?"

Positive Traits among Adolescents

On the road to adulthood, adolescents often demonstrate a number of exceptional qualities we all can learn from. Four stand out in particular. First, there is *a willingness to risk*—to abandon what is safe and secure and to relocate into new and unfamiliar territory. Second, there is *a sensitivity to God*—to let His Word take root in their lives, to grow in Christ, and to yield the Spirit's fruit. Third, there is *a commitment to integrity*—to hold to their ideals and consistently live out their convictions. Fourth, there is *a determination to stand*—to deepen their individual roots and withstand the hurricane-force pressure of their peers.

Scriptural Examples of These Traits

Four teenagers in the Bible especially demonstrate these valuable traits: Isaac, Samuel, Josiah, and Daniel.

This lesson has been adapted from the study guide *Growing Wise in Family Life*, coauthored by Ken Gire, from the Bible-teaching ministry of Charles R. Swindoll (Fullerton, Calif.: Insight for Living, 1988), pp. 89–92.

Isaac

When his parents were well past their childbearing years, God promised them a son. He also promised Abraham and Sarah that through this son—Isaac—He would make a great nation that would be a blessing to the entire earth (Gen. 12:1–3; 17:15–19). But when this promised son became a teenager, God threw Abraham a major league curveball.

> Now it came about after these things, that God tested Abraham, and said to him, "Abraham!" And he said, "Here I am." And He said, "Take now your son, your only son, whom you love, Isaac, and go to the land of Moriah; and offer him there as a burnt offering on one of the mountains of which I will tell you." (22:1–2)

Remarkably, Abraham offered no resistance.

> And Abraham took the wood of the burnt offering and laid it on Isaac his son, and he took in his hand the fire and the knife. So the two of them walked on together. And Isaac spoke to Abraham his father and said, "My father!" And he said, "Here I am, my son." And he said, "Behold, the fire and the wood, but where is the lamb for the burnt offering?" And Abraham said, "God will provide for Himself the lamb for the burnt offering, my son." So the two of them walked on together. (vv. 6–8)

Like his father, Isaac was also willing to submit himself to the will of God, however incomprehensible, however inscrutable. It was a step of faith, a risk that could cost him his life. But a risk he calculated as worth taking.

> Then they came to the place of which God had told him; and Abraham built the altar there, and arranged the wood, and bound his son Isaac, and laid him on the altar on top of the wood. And Abraham stretched out his hand, and took the knife to slay his son. But the angel of the Lord called to him from heaven, and said, "Abraham, Abraham!" And he said, "Here I am." And he said, "Do not stretch out your hand against the lad, and do nothing to

him; for now I know that you fear God, since you have not withheld your son, your only son, from Me." (vv. 9–12)

The youthful willingness to risk—that's the strength of Isaac! As we grow older, this adventurous spirit so often gives way to a cautious, stay-in-the-shallow-end mentality. We cling to the security of what we know rather than open our arms to new challenges. How much we can learn from the Isaacs around us, who trust God and give Him everything without reservation. As the apostle Paul wrote,

> I urge you therefore, brethren, by the mercies of God, to present your bodies a living and holy sacrifice, acceptable to God, which is your spiritual service of worship. (Rom. 12:1)

Will you follow Isaac onto the altar?

Samuel

Placed in Eli's custodial care at an early age, Samuel was raised in a less than ideal home (1 Sam. 1:1–2:36). Eli was a successful priest but an abysmal parent. His two sons blatantly rebelled, bringing shame to their father and to their priestly profession (2:12–17, 22–25). Samuel, however, stood in bold contrast.

> Now the boy Samuel was ministering to the Lord before Eli. And word from the Lord was rare in those days, visions were infrequent. And it happened at that time as Eli was lying down in his place (now his eyesight had begun to grow dim and he could not see well), and the lamp of God had not yet gone out, and Samuel was lying down in the temple of the Lord where the ark of God was. . . .
>
> Then the Lord came and stood and called as at other times, "Samuel! Samuel!" And Samuel said, "Speak, for Thy servant is listening." (3:1–3, 10)

We can see that young Samuel was responsive and quick to hear God's word. And because he, with a little help from Eli, had cultivated this quality in his youth, when he matured he was still sensitive to God.

> Thus Samuel grew and the Lord was with him

and let none of his words fail. And all Israel from Dan even to Beersheba knew that Samuel was confirmed as a prophet of the Lord. And the Lord appeared again at Shiloh, because the Lord revealed Himself to Samuel at Shiloh by the word of the Lord. (vv. 19–21)

Sensitivity and submissiveness to God's voice are two traits that should be stamped "FRAGILE." En route to adulthood, it's easy for these qualities to become dented or broken as they travel over the uncertain road of adolescence. And often, when we finally reach maturity, those are the boxes that are inadvertently left behind or somehow lost in transit. So if you or someone you know is trafficking through the spiritual teenage years, put a little extra padding around those two boxes . . . and be sure to mark them "HANDLE WITH CARE."

Josiah

Prior to Josiah's reign, leadership was at low tide in Judah. King Manasseh had reigned fifty-five years and done "evil in the sight of the Lord" (2 Chron. 33:1–9). His son Amon succeeded him and followed the same corrupt path (vv. 21–23). After Amon was assassinated, his young son Josiah was placed on the throne (vv. 24–25). But Josiah did not practice idolatry or immorality as did his predecessors. Instead, he committed himself to integrity. Let's take a look at his character.

Josiah was eight years old when he became king, and he reigned thirty-one years in Jerusalem. And he did right in the sight of the Lord, and walked in the ways of his father David and did not turn aside to the right or to the left. For in the eighth year of his reign while he was still a youth, he began to seek the God of his father David; and in the twelfth year he began to purge Judah and Jerusalem of the high places, the Asherim, the carved images, and the molten images. And they tore down the altars of the Baals in his presence, and the incense altars that were high above them he chopped down; also the Asherim, the carved images, and the molten images he broke in pieces and ground to powder and scattered it on the graves of those who had sacrificed to them. Then he burned the bones of the priests on their altars, and purged Judah and Jerusalem. (34:1–5)

The fires of this cathartic purge were fanned from the flames of his passion for God—a passion that ignited when he was just sixteen.

Daniel

Another teenager whose character exemplified something right about adolescence was Daniel. Remember his story? In the Babylonian captivity, Judah was deported and taken into bondage by King Nebuchadnezzar (Dan. 1:1–2). But the king took a handful of Israel's brightest teenagers and gave them an intensive, three-year crash course in Babylonian culture (vv. 3–5). Part of the indoctrination was culinary, but some of the food was in violation of the Mosaic dietary regulations. It was on this issue that Daniel was determined to take a stand.

> But Daniel made up his mind that he would not defile himself with the king's choice food or with the wine which he drank; so he sought permission from the commander of the officials that he might not defile himself. (v. 8)

It was a gutsy stand—a stand that helped put gristle in his spiritual life. And it was a stand that would later help give him the courage to step into the lions' den (Dan. 6).

A Thought for the Road

The four teenagers we've studied exhibit extraordinary qualities of spiritual maturity. They demonstrate that the move from adolescence—whether literal or spiritual—to adulthood doesn't have to scratch and dent the character along the way. Paul's words to the young pastor Timothy leave us with a few tips to ensure safe passage:

> Let no one look down on your youthfulness, but rather in speech, conduct, love, faith and purity, show yourself an example of those who believe. (1 Tim. 4:12)

Living Insights

Like teenagers, adolescent Christians are a complex blend of contrasts. For instance, compare our descriptions of them from chapter 9 with our points in this chapter:

Chapter 9 "Adolescents in Adult Bodies"	Chapter 11 "What's *Right* about Adolescence?"
Instability when the way gets rough	Willingness to risk
Insensitivity when the will gets challenged	Sensitivity to God
Irresponsibility when the world gets appealing	Commitment to integrity; determination to stand

Which set of characteristics is accurate? How should we paint adolescent believers—with harsh lines or flowing curves? With dark tones or pastels?

The answer is: both.

If you're in this stage of spiritual growth, or if you intimately know someone in this stage, you understand what we mean. One week, adolescent Christians are ready to pitch their faith; but the next week, they're signing up to follow Christ to the ends of the earth. One day, they're playfully tagging along with the world; and the next, they're standing for God with determination.

Jesus' disciples rode that same roller coaster of faith, didn't they? One night they said they'd die for Christ, but when the soldiers came, "they all left Him and fled" (Mark 14:50). But look how they turned out. They eventually leveled their mountains and valleys into a consistent walk with Him.

If your faith has had its ups and downs, don't get frustrated with yourself. Keep going. Paul says Christ's patience is "unlimited" (1 Tim. 1:16 NIV)—just the kind of patience every teenager needs from a parent.

And if you know adolescent Christians, how patient with them have you been lately? How encouraging?

Each of the teenagers in our study displayed their unique strengths in response to a test. Isaac was tested on the altar of obedience; Samuel, in an unhealthy family environment; Josiah, during an era of national wickedness; and Daniel, under the weight of peer pressure.

Are you enduring a test right now? Perhaps it concerns your health or finances or family. Maybe the world is luring you into compromise. Or maybe you're enduring a period of self-doubt and fear. What is your test and which of the strengths from our study do you need at this time?

❏ Willingness to submit your will and take a risk

❏ Sensitivity to hear and respond to God's voice

❏ Commitment to integrity

❏ Determination to stand against the crowd

_____

_____

_____

In every trial there is a watershed moment. Will you give in to something or stand up to it? Play or fold? Stay or leave? The choice can be difficult. Perhaps, though, now is the time to decide what you're going to do. We've provided you some space to record your resolution. And remember: God will give you the unique strength you need to pass this test.

_____

_____

_____

_____

Chapter 12

REASONS WE RESIST
BECOMING MATURE

Hebrews 2:1–3; 3:12–13; 4:1–2; 5:11–14

Study hard in school, and it's possible to skip a grade. But no matter how hard children try—and they do try—they can't skip an age or a stage in the growth process. No amount of wishing can make a seven-year-old turn thirteen overnight. And no child can leap into adulthood without first careening through puberty.

Puberty—that highway of hormones in overdrive! Navigating through adolescence is certainly no Sunday drive in the country. There are dangerous curves and confusing intersections along the road to maturity, and some people who should be adults because of their age are still lost in the stage of adolescence.

Spiritually, some Christians fail to reach maturity too, but not for lack of guidance or power. They simply choose to pull over and enjoy the status quo. But God wants us to move on in our faith, as Paul exhorts:

> We are no longer to be children, . . . but speaking the truth in love, we are to grow up in all aspects into Him, who is the head, even Christ. (Eph. 4:14a, 15)

Yet something within us resists growing up. Physically, as children, we couldn't wait to grow up. So why do we resist it spiritually?

Our search for reasons begins with a few simple observations about human nature.

A Time for Honest Confession

If we're honest, we can probably list a few characteristics about ourselves that naturally conflict with growth. First, *we're creatures of habit*. And, as the saying goes, "Old habits die hard." We prefer the easy-chair comfort of our familiar patterns of thinking and acting. Exchanging them for new and healthier habits is just plain hard work.

Second, *we want a Savior, not a Master*. We'd rather revel in the thoughts of Jesus snatching us from the jaws of hell and winging us to heaven than be confronted by His often uncomfortable commands as Lord to leave our nets and follow Him.

Third, *we tend to stop short of our potential.* Most of us choose the path of least resistance, avoiding the challenges that would stretch our capacities. For example, although our brains have the capacity for amazing memory, we rarely use them to their full capability. Similarly, in the spiritual realm, we often run out of steam before becoming all God wants us to be.

Again, the question is: Why? What makes us so rooted in habit, resistant to God's authority, and rutted in the status quo? What keeps us from attaining the maturity Christ has in mind for us? The writer to the Hebrews pinpointed among his readers some causes of spiritual lethargy that still hold true today.

A Letter with Relevant Information

Times were tough for the Hebrew believers. And the author of this letter was concerned that they would waste away in their faith without the spiritual muscle that comes with maturity. Simply put, his message to them was,

> Therefore leaving the elementary teaching about the Christ, *let us press on to maturity.* (Heb. 6:1a, emphasis added)

But maturity was eluding them—and often eludes us—for four reasons.

1. Because We Drift Away from What We Hear

> For this reason we must pay much closer attention to what we have heard, lest we drift away from it. For if the word spoken through angels proved unalterable, and every transgression and disobedience received a just recompense, how shall we escape if we neglect so great a salvation? After it was at the first spoken through the Lord, it was confirmed to us by those who heard. (Heb. 2:1–3)

The first cause for our stunted growth is that we tend to drift away from what we hear, neglecting the truth. It's not as if we're deaf to God's Word; we listen to it, but we disregard it. We store it safely on a shelf in our minds, while distractions lure our attention elsewhere.

The writer to the Hebrews uses a telling word picture in the phrases "drift away" (*pararrein* in the Greek) and "pay much closer attention to" (*prosechein*), as William Barclay reveals.

> Both these words have also a nautical sense. *Prosechein* can mean *to moor a ship;* and *pararrein* can be used of a ship which has been carelessly allowed to slip past a harbour or a haven because the mariner has forgotten to allow for the wind or the current or the tide. So, then, this first verse could be very vividly translated: "Therefore, we must the more eagerly anchor our lives to the things that we have been taught lest the ship of life drift past the harbour and be wrecked." It is a vivid picture of a ship drifting to destruction because the pilot sleeps.[1]

Barclay continues, elaborating on the dangers of drifting.

> For most of us the threat of life is not so much that we should plunge into disaster, but that we should drift into sin. There are few people who deliberately and in a moment turn their backs on God; there are many who day by day drift farther and farther away from him. There are not many who in one moment of time commit some disastrous sin; there are many who almost imperceptibly involve themselves in some situation and suddenly awake to find that they have ruined life for themselves and broken someone else's heart. We must be continually on the alert against the peril of the drifting life.[2]

This peril can lead to an even more treacherous danger.

2. Because We Fall Aside

> Take care, brethren, lest there should be in any one of you an evil, unbelieving heart, in falling away from the living God. But encourage one another day after day, as long as it is still called "Today," lest any one of you be hardened by the deceitfulness of sin. (3:12–13)

1. William Barclay, *The Letter to the Hebrews*, rev. ed., The Daily Study Bible Series (Philadelphia, Pa.: Westminster Press, 1976), p. 21.

2. Barclay, *The Letter to the Hebrews*, p. 21.

Another reason we resist growth is that we sometimes fall aside from the Lord's path for our lives. And, like the Israelites, we begin wandering in our own wildernesses of sin (see vv. 7–11). Remember their story? They were suffering as slaves when the Lord led them out of Egypt and set them on a journey to the Promised Land— about a month-long trip that lasted forty years. Why the meandering detours?

> It wasn't because the Israelites had lost their map; it was because they had lost their way. The root of their waywardness was a heart condition. They had hearts that had lost their tenderness and grown tough. Hearts that had lost their responsiveness and become rough. Calloused to God's revelation. Cavalier to His warnings.[3]

Heart disease doesn't happen all at once. Over time, sin deceives us with promises it can't deliver. It convinces us that feeling good is more important than the truth and that the world's majority opinion must be right. We begin thinking, *Who needs that out-of-date scriptural stuff, anyway?* Sunday after Sunday, week after week, we hear the truth, but our hearts become hardened with unbelief. Eventually, we fall aside.

What guards us from losing our way? Mutual encouragement, according to the writer to the Hebrews. Mature believers can help us see the faultiness of our thinking and keep our hearts soft to the truth.

3. Because We Fail to Mix Faith with Truth

> Therefore, let us fear lest, while a promise remains of entering His rest, any one of you should seem to have come short of it. For indeed we have had good news preached to us, just as they also; but the word they heard did not profit them, because it was not united by faith in those who heard. (4:1–2)

We can summarize the writer's third reason with his phrase: "the word they heard . . . was not united by faith." Truth in the mind must link up with the hands and feet of faith, or else it is

---

3. From the study guide *The Preeminent Person of Christ: A Study of Hebrews 1–10*, coauthored by Ken Gire, from the Bible-teaching ministry of Charles R. Swindoll (Fullerton, Calif.: Insight for Living, 1989), p. 55.

useless to help us grow.

We may have memorized ten verses against greed and impatience, but if we still live for riches and snap at everyone who makes a mistake, we aren't growing. We may sit under the finest teachers and hear the grandest sermons, but we won't mature in Christ until we apply what we know.

Someone once said, "The Bible was not given to satisfy idle curiosity; it was given to change a life." Even a little knowledge of the truth can go a long way toward our maturity if we mix it thoroughly with practical faith and action.

4. Because We Become Dull of Hearing

So far, each reason for resisting growth has taken us down, down, down. We hear the truth, but we drift away from it. We hear the truth, but because of sin we fall aside. We hear the truth, but it makes no difference in our lives. It makes sense, then, that eventually we stop hearing altogether.

> Concerning him we have much to say, and it is hard to explain, since you have become dull of hearing. For though by this time you ought to be teachers, you have need again for someone to teach you the elementary principles of the oracles of God, and you have come to need milk and not solid food. For everyone who partakes only of milk is not accustomed to the word of righteousness, for he is a babe. But solid food is for the mature, who because of practice have their senses trained to discern good and evil. (5:11–14)

As long as we have our spiritual hearing, we have hope. But when we become dull of hearing, the truth passes us by. Can you imagine a worse fate?

Think of the many channels God uses to communicate with us. He speaks to us in the music of worship, in the prayers, and in the fellowship. Through His Word, He guides us; through the heights and depths of our emotions, He loves us. He teaches us faith in life's failures, grace in our successes. And in our suffering, He teaches us to obey. According to the writer to the Hebrews, Christ Himself "learned obedience from the things which He suffered" (5:8).

But these channels are severed when we become dull of hearing.

97

Still longing for contact with God, yet without spiritual hearing, we grope through our suffering searching for meaning and finding only silence. Is there any greater human pain?

A Final Thought

To soften our resistance to spiritual growth so we can "press on to maturity," we offer the oil of this simple thought: *stay teachable.* God will use every circumstance to help you mature if you lean forward and listen for His voice. What could He be teaching you in your marriage? Your business? Your suffering? Listen. But listen with your heart *and* your hands; with the truth, mix a little faith. And stay teachable.

 Living Insights STUDY ONE

Over the past twenty years, I figure I've listened to about nine hundred Sunday morning sermons and sat through at least as many Sunday school lessons and Bible study lectures. Christian teachers have wowed me, wooed me, and walloped me with God's Word. Their books and notebooks line my shelves like tin soldiers, ready to battle heresy and lead me to spiritual victory. Yet I sometimes wonder how much of this steady barrage of truth has sunk into my heart and how much has skittered across the surface like pebbles on a frozen lake.

If we're not careful, our hearts can become hardened to the constant input of truth. While listening to a sermon, we can get that glazed, "I've-heard-this-before" look as we sit back for a half-hour mental siesta. Or we can treat scriptural truths like collectibles, neatly gathering and storing them for display. All the while, though, the flame in our heart is slowly sputtering out.

Have you sensed a chill of spiritual apathy gripping your soul? Are you resistant to growth—maybe not actively but with passive indifference? Perhaps this lesson has uncovered the causes of resistance in your life:

Drifting away from what you hear
Falling aside from God's path
Failing to mix faith with truth
Becoming dull of hearing

If so, take a few moments to write down specifically what is turning your heart cold and keeping you from growing.

_____

_____

_____

_____

By developing a teachable spirit you can begin warming up your spiritual enthusiasm. Let's explore this idea in the next Living Insights.

 Living Insights   STUDY TWO

Webster's defines *teachable* as "capable of being taught; apt and willing to learn."[4] That definition is true, of course, but it lacks heart. Listen to the prayer of a Mississippi country preacher who captures the spirit of what it really means to be "apt and willing to learn":

> "Oh, Lord, give thy servant this mornin' the eyes of the eagle and the wisdom of the owl; connect his soul with the gospel telephone in the central skies; illuminate his brow with the Sun of Heaven; possess his mind with love for the people; turpentine his imagination, grease his lips with possum oil; electrify his brain with the lightnin' of the Word; put perpetual motion in his arms; fill him plumb full of dynamite of Thy glory; anoint him all over with the kerosene of salvation, and set him on fire. Amen!"[5]

There's no dullness in his spiritual hearing! He's seeking the Lord with his whole heart. He's hungering and thirsting for righteousness. He's ready to respond to God's truth with explosive obedience. He's *teachable*.

Teachable King David expressed his willingness to learn and

---

4. *Merriam-Webster's Collegiate Dictionary*, 10th ed., see "teachable."

5. From a story by William J. Bausch, *Storytelling, Imagination and Faith* (Mystic, Conn.: Twenty-Third Publications, 1984), p. 141; as quoted by Brennan Manning in *The Signature of Jesus on the Pages of Our Lives* (Portland, Oreg.: Multnomah Press, 1992), p. 89.

grow in the Psalms. Meditate on the following prayers that he wrote; then, in the space provided, express your own desire for the Lord to anoint you "all over with the kerosene of salvation" and set you on fire!

Psalm 25:4–5   Psalm 86:11–13

Psalm 63:1–5   Psalm 119:33–40

_____

_____

_____

_____

_____

Chapter 13

THE CHURCH:
WHO NEEDS IT?

Selected Scriptures

While growing up in our faith, we sometimes go through periods in which we question the value of the local—or, as some would put it, institutional—church. We want to serve Christ on our own without getting entangled in building funds and pipe organs and padded pews, which seem to just distract us from our main purpose: spreading the gospel. In the marketplace with non-Christians is where we ought to be, right? Not preaching to ourselves in stained-glass cathedrals.

These feelings raise a legitimate question: Do we really need the church?

In this chapter, we won't try to strong-arm you into a certain answer; instead, we simply want to paint the church from God's palette of colors and, hopefully, stir in you an appreciation for the contribution it can make in your life.

People's Comments about the Church

Opinions about the church vary from person to person, but we can boil down most people's comments into three categories: their views on the church's identity, their criticisms, and their expectations.

Concerning the church's identity, many people view it as nothing more than big business. Others idealize it as a center for evangelism or a hospital for the needy. Still others see it simply as a nice addition to the community—a good place to mingle, make business contacts, meet people.

Criticism comes in all shapes and sizes: the church is too rigid; it's too lax; it's lost touch with the world; it doesn't meet my inner needs; and, of course, it's full of hypocrites.

But perhaps people's harshest criticisms of the church arise from their unmet expectations. Some people expect it to take a strong stand on issues, while others say it should be more compassionate. Some believe the church should strengthen its political arm, while others decry its involvement in politics. Some count on their church staying intimate and comfortable, while others hope their church will grow, grow, grow!

More than anything, though, most people yearn to be part of a church that cares about people. "What my spirit reaches out for," confides one author,

> is that group of people who accept me as I am— warts and all! I'm looking for that support team. I'm looking for that kind of encouragement. I'm looking for a church body that won't always knock me dead with scripture or spiritualize everything in life. And tell me, aren't you looking for the same thing?[1]

"Yes!" we cry—especially those among us who still bear the emotional wounds from bad experiences with the church.

Whatever our situation or opinion, we all agree that the Person who can give us the best perspective of the church is its founder and chief supporter—Jesus Christ.

Christ's Statement on the Church

Christ broke ground for the church with these words to Peter:

> "And I also say to you that you are Peter, and upon this rock I will build My church; and the gates of Hades shall not overpower it." (Matt. 16:18)

To gain a deeper understanding of what Jesus is saying, let's break this verse down into three sections.

First: The Project Is Christ's

Underscore in your mind the words, "I will build." Christ is the construction supervisor. With the Father's blueprints in hand, He directs the work according to His specifications, not ours. We err by thinking that we're the ones in charge and that the church's completion depends on us. Jesus alone is the master architect.

Second: The Church Belongs to Him

"I will build My church," Christ continues. It belongs to Him. And as its owner, He focuses His full attention on maintaining and defending it.

1. Luci Swindoll, *The Alchemy of the Heart* (Portland, Oreg.: Multnomah Press, 1984), p. 170.

Third: It Will Survive, Regardless

Even "the gates of Hades shall not overpower it." If the church wasn't so precious to the Lord, He might let it slowly sag and crumble, like an aging farmhouse. But it is His most prized possession, and though the legions of hell should besiege it, the church will stand forever.

All this leads us to an important conclusion: If the church is that valuable to Christ, should we value it any less? Should we treat lightly the very thing He gave His life to own, build, and protect? And it makes us wonder: What is it about this vessel of clay that elicits His love? Throughout its history, the church has sullied His name more than honored it. Why does He stand by it so faithfully?

Christ is committed to it, not because He's committed to an institution, but because He's committed to us. The word *church* in Greek, *ekklēsia*, means literally "called-out ones." The church is a body, not a building. We don't *go* to church; we *are* the church.

We can think of ourselves as the church in a universal sense or a local sense. The universal church is "the whole company of the redeemed throughout this present era," while the local church is a subset of believers who meet together in a certain area.[2]

Both concepts are important. Spiritual birth gives us immediate entrance into the universal church, much like natural birth ushers us into the human race. But the local church provides us the family context in which we mature. Trying to grow up in Christ apart from the local church is like attempting to raise yourself from infancy without parents.

Christ instituted the church because we need a family. We need a place where our children can become rooted in the faith and our teenagers can discover how Christ fits into their lives. We need a place to join together—to laugh, to grieve, to learn, to grow. And we need a place where we can follow spiritual models, who, like shepherds, can watch over us wandering sheep (see Acts 20:28).

Perhaps the church's greatest shepherd was the apostle Paul. As we seek to understand the value of the church, let's ask him why he was so passionately committed to the local churches of his day.

2. W. E. Vine, *Vine's Expository Dictionary of Old and New Testament Words* (Old Tappan, N.J.: Fleming H. Revell Co., 1981), p. 84.

Paul's Commitment to the Church

In his New Testament letters, Paul lists several reasons. We'll choose only four here, the first being from his epistle to the Romans.

Healthy Relationships

> For just as we have many members in one body and all the members do not have the same function, so we, who are many, are one body in Christ, and individually members one of another. And since we have gifts that differ according to the grace given to us, let each exercise them accordingly: if prophecy, according to the proportion of his faith; if service, in his serving; or he who teaches, in his teaching; or he who exhorts, in his exhortation; he who gives, with liberality; he who leads, with diligence; he who shows mercy, with cheerfulness.
>
> Let love be without hypocrisy. Abhor what is evil; cling to what is good. Be devoted to one another in brotherly love; give preference to one another in honor; not lagging behind in diligence, fervent in spirit, serving the Lord; rejoicing in hope, persevering in tribulation, devoted to prayer, contributing to the needs of the saints, practicing hospitality. (Rom. 12:4–13)

In the church, we're "members one of another," implying both community and accountability (vv. 4–5). Your neighborhood may provide you a sense of community, but much more intimate is the fellowship among like-minded believers. Your employer can hold you accountable, but not to the same personal level as your Christian brothers and sisters can.

Also, we express our gifts and serve one another in the church as we teach and exhort and show mercy to each other (see vv. 6–8). And it is here that we find the two most precious commodities, love and acceptance (see vv. 9–11).

Finally, the church offers emotional support and spiritual care (see vv. 12–14). During hard times, who else can we turn to for the strength that prayers from fellow Christians can offer?

Unity and Compassion

Paul calculates the precious value of the church's unity and compassion in 1 Corinthians 12:24b–26.

> God has so composed the body, giving more abun-
> dant honor to that member which lacked, that there
> should be no division in the body, but that the mem-
> bers should have the same care for one another. And
> if one member suffers, all the members suffer with
> it; if one member is honored, all the members rejoice
> with it.

Do you feel that same compassion at your work? At school? In your neighborhood? Usually, people are too busy to suffer when you suffer or rejoice when you rejoice. But God designed His church to be as interconnected as the limbs on your body. How sad when believers sever themselves from the church, thinking they don't need the support of other Christians. How much better it is to share our heartaches and victories and to receive the nourishment only a body can give.

Consistent Generosity

In another letter to the Corinthians, the Apostle applauds the Macedonian churches for their willingness to financially help their poorer members.

> Now, brethren, we wish to make known to you
> the grace of God which has been given in the
> churches of Macedonia, that in a great ordeal of
> affliction their abundance of joy and their deep pov-
> erty overflowed in the wealth of their liberality. For
> I testify that according to their ability, and beyond
> their ability they gave of their own accord, begging
> us with much entreaty for the favor of participation
> in the support of the saints, and this, not as we had
> expected, but they first gave themselves to the Lord
> and to us by the will of God. (2 Cor. 8:1–5)

These believers, who were themselves impoverished, *begged* Paul to take their money and give it to the Christians who needed it most. Sadly, in our day, some church leaders have played the char-latan, padding their pockets with donations intended for ministry. Because of their lack of integrity, all ministries have suffered. For by stealing our money, they stole our joy of giving as well. Christ never had this kind of leader in mind for His church. If you find a ministry you can trust, though, you'll discover the true thrill of giving.

Liberty, Love, and Serving

Finally, to the Galatian believers Paul explains how our liberty in Christ expresses itself in love and service.

> It was for freedom that Christ set us free; therefore keep standing firm and do not be subject again to a yoke of slavery. . . .
> For you were called to freedom, brethren; only do not turn your freedom into an opportunity for the flesh, but through love serve one another. For the whole Law is fulfilled in one word, in the statement, "You shall love your neighbor as yourself." But if you bite and devour one another, take care lest you be consumed by one another. (Gal. 5:1, 13–15)

Christ said, "My yoke is easy, and My load is light" (Matt. 11:30). But some churches find it their duty to press Christ's yoke hard against our shoulders, causing us to stumble under a heavy load of regulations. Minor issues suddenly become the measure of our spirituality, and we soon begin to "bite and devour" each other with critical comments and judgmental attitudes.

God, however, designed the church to be a hall of liberty, where we are free to worship without fear of condemnation. Of course, Paul wasn't saying that Christ's liberty bell emancipates our flesh to do whatever it wants. Instead, Christ has set us free to serve one another, gladly bearing His yoke of love.

Practically speaking, what do Paul's reasons for committing himself to the church mean to us? Let's list them on a ledger in modern terms, so we can total them up for ourselves.

The church is where:

✓ children are nurtured and loved

✓ teenagers discover wisdom

✓ adults find refuge, hope, courage, and reproof

✓ worship is sent heavenward

✓ our hunger for God is satisfied

✓ our finances are used for eternal good

✓ we become aware of God's world program

✓ our families are equipped, challenged, and strengthened

✓ hurting people find understanding and affirmation

Our Involvement in the Church

Do these attributes add up to a desire to get more involved in your church? Many churches offer membership as an expression of commitment to a local body of believers. The following is a list of expectations the First Evangelical Free Church of Fullerton, California, Chuck Swindoll's home church for more than twenty years, holds for its members:

1. Assume responsibility for his or her own spiritual nourishment through personal and corporate Bible study and prayer.

2. Participate in the weekly worship services on a regular basis.

3. Join the family life of the church in a congregational and/or small group context.

4. Exercise his or her spiritual gifts in specific areas of involvement.

5. Support the variety of ministries of the church through prayer and service.

6. Contribute financially to our church in a consistent, generous manner.

7. Share his or her faith personally while supporting others who proclaim the gospel around the world.

8. Respond positively to the leadership of the Elder Board in matters of church policy and discipline.

If you haven't already, won't you consider committing yourself to a local family of believers? It's a great place to grow up.

Are you looking for a church right now? If you've been church-hunting for very long, you know how confusing it can be. There are so many different denominations and styles of worship. How do you know which one is the best for you and your family?

Insight for Living publishes a pamphlet titled "How to Recognize a Healthy Church," and you can write to us to receive your free copy. The following summarizes its highlights.

When you visit a church, the first thing you'll notice is its personality. It may resemble a theater, emphasizing music and drama. Or it may remind you of a town square, where the Good News of the King is heralded. Perhaps it will resemble a hospital or a family center. Any one of these types may appeal to you, but we encourage you to look a little deeper and check the church's vital signs—six qualities that reveal its true health.

1. *A healthy church glorifies God.* Does the church emphasize its own greatness or God's greatness?

2. *A healthy church worships God with a genuine spirit of devotion.* Does the spirit in which the songs are sung and Scriptures opened lift your soul to heaven?

3. *A healthy church balances biblical instruction with personal application.* Is the church breathing Scripture in and out—*in* the people's minds through solid teaching and *out* their hands and feet through practical application?

4. *A healthy church exudes warmth.* Do people seem to be involved in each other's lives?

5. *A healthy church reaches out to others.* Is this church equipping believers to meet the world's needs? Are non-Christians treated with respect?

6. *A healthy church has a contagious style.* Before you leave, give the church one last look up and down. Is it biblical in its teaching? Authentic in nature? Gracious in attitude? Relevant in approach? This kind of church will draw growing Christians like a magnet.

Keep this list of qualities in mind as you attend church this Sunday. Even if you're not looking for a new church, you can use it to give your current one a quick checkup. Certainly, no church is perfect, but overall, you should be able to tell which ones have a clean bill of health.

 Living Insights

Let's end this chapter with a spin on the question we started with: Why should I go to church? Some Christians go to church to avoid the "guilties." Others attend out of duty. Others go . . . just because!

Why do you go to church? As you consider your reasons, compare them with some of the main points in the lesson. Do you, perhaps, need to reevaluate your motives for being involved in church? If so, in what ways?

_____

_____

_____

_____

_____

How can you make going to church more meaningful for yourself and your family?

_____

_____

_____

_____

_____

Chapter 14

A STORY FOR ADULTS
TO REMEMBER

2 Samuel 24:10–25

The Old Testament world is a wonderland for children. It's a place where floating arks keep animals safe during storms, and rainbows remind us everything's going to be all right. In this faraway land, a little girl like Esther can grow up to become queen. A little boy like Samuel can speak with God in the night. And neighborhood bullies like Goliath get what's coming to them.

But the Old Testament isn't just for kids. It's for adults too. In fact, it's the best place to learn what being a spiritual adult is all about. Surprised? Often, as we come of age, we graduate to the abstract concepts of the New Testament, relegating the Old Testament to children's Sunday school. However, if the apostle Paul were here, he'd advise us not to pack away the old flannel-graph stories so soon. They have a lot to teach us about Christian maturity, perhaps more than we think.

A Reminder: The Reason for Old Testament Stories

Paul unveils the precious value contained within the Old Testament in his letter to the Romans:

> Whatever was written in earlier times was written for our instruction, that through perseverance and the encouragement of the Scriptures we might have hope. (15:4)

Studying the Jewish stories is more than just gathering historical trivia. The early writings are "for our instruction." They provide us a course no university offers—Life 101. In this class, according to professor Paul, we learn

perseverance—the ability to hold up under stress;
encouragement—the stability gained by courage within; and
hope—the capability to remain full of faith.

So come along with us into the world of the Old Testament for a while. It may take a moment to get our bearings, because here

God doesn't teach His lessons using the familiar New Testament didactic style. Instead, He uses real-life drama, sweeping landscapes, and Shakespearean dilemmas—as in this story from the life of aging King David.

A Story: The Maturity of an Ancient King

The winter sky is beginning to cast shadows across David as he enters the final season of his life and reign. From tending sheep to shepherding a nation, this man of God has scaled the heights of greatness. We would expect him to be basking in the sunset glow of his accomplishments. But, once again falling victim to his own human frailty, he has entered another dark valley. "While David was faithful to the end, he was also fallible to the end," observes commentator Charles Gulston.[1] For, against wise counsel, David has decided to number the people of Israel.

Taking a census—what's wrong with that? Gulston explains why it was sin:

> The offense in this instance was the motive behind it. David was filled with a sudden desire to glory in Israel's military strength. There was a strong element of pride in this desire which struck at the very root of the nation's life style, its utter dependence on God.[2]

It seems strange for a man of David's character to be proud. He should have known better. Certainly, if we were king, we wouldn't have yearned to glory in our own strength, right?

Well . . . maybe.

Oh, all right, we probably would have let our pride get the better of us too. In fact, that's why we like David so much—he's just like us. And his example instructs us that, no matter how old or successful or close to God we are, we're never immune to temptation.

But this story is only beginning. There's so much more to learn! What David does after he sins is the true measure of his maturity; for it's not our ability to be perfect but how we respond to our own sin that reveals our maturity level. In the events that follow, David demonstrates four characteristics of spiritual adulthood.

---

1. Charles Gulston, *David: Shepherd and King* (Grand Rapids, Mich.: Zondervan Publishing House, 1980), p. 187.
2. Gulston, *David: Shepherd and King*, p. 187.

A Mature Conscience

For more than nine months, David's right-hand man, Joab, has traveled the country, counting the people. Upon his return, he spreads out a banquet of figures before the king:

> There were in Israel eight hundred thousand valiant men who drew the sword, and the men of Judah were five hundred thousand men. (2 Sam. 24:9b)

The deed is done. Pride's appetite is satisfied. But that night, the king experiences spiritual heartburn.

> Now David's heart troubled him after he had numbered the people. (v. 10a)

The Hebrew word for "troubled," *nakah*, is a violent word meaning "smite, strike, hit, beat, slay, kill." [3] Stricken with guilt, David's heart battles his pride until, finally, he surrenders and confesses his sin:

> "I have sinned greatly in what I have done. But now, O Lord, please take away the iniquity of Thy servant, for I have acted very foolishly." (v. 10b)

Can you imagine a king saying he "acted very foolishly"? Kings don't have to admit their mistakes. They're accountable to no one. And if a disaster does occur, they can blame it on someone else. Not this king, however. He submitted to his inner judge, his conscience. And he humbly followed as his guilt led him to repentance.

The first characteristic of maturity is a *sensitive conscience*. Spiritual adults don't look for scapegoats when they sin. They own their mistakes. They listen to the late-night churnings within their hearts. And they're willing to say, "I was wrong."

A Mature Mind

When the sun's early morning rays break the darkness, David arises forgiven. But he also awakes to the reality of sin's consequences—which strides into his throne room dressed in prophet's garb.

> When David arose in the morning, the word of the Lord came to the prophet Gad, David's seer, saying,

---

3. R. Laird Harris, Gleason L. Archer, Jr., and Bruce K. Waltke, eds., *Theological Wordbook of the Old Testament* (Chicago, Ill.: Moody Press, 1980), vol. 2, p. 577.

"Go and speak to David, 'Thus the Lord says, "I am offering you three things; choose for yourself one of them, which I may do to you."'" So Gad came to David and told him, and said to him, "Shall seven years of famine come to you in your land? Or will you flee three months before your foes while they pursue you? Or shall there be three days' pestilence in your land? Now consider and see what answer I shall return to Him who sent me." Then David said to Gad, "I am in great distress." (vv. 11–14a)

David painfully realizes that he cannot fall without the people he loves getting hurt. And because, as a leader, he has greater responsibility, God makes him issue the death order himself, bearing the full weight of his sin. Oh, the agony of this moment! But while his heart is breaking, his mind is thinking maturely, and he makes the wisest choice:

"Let us now fall into the hand of the Lord for His mercies are great, but do not let me fall into the hand of man." (v. 14b)

Here David models the second characteristic of the spiritual adult: *a mind that thinks theologically.* He made his decision based on his understanding of the nature of God versus the nature of man. God's mercies are great. Although He may discipline us, once the sin is dealt with, it is forgotten. People, though, tend to hang on to past wrongs and take revenge. So David chose three days under God's judgment rather than three months under his enemy's sword.

A side point: notice that David made his decision by himself. Although mature people understand the importance of relationships, they also realize that sometimes they must walk certain dark valleys alone with God.

A Mature Attitude

Having made his choice, David can do nothing but await the coming storm. For three days, a pestilence ravages the people and, because of David's sin, thousands die. But just as the angel of death stands poised to afflict the people of Jerusalem, God halts him by the threshing floor owned by a man named Araunah (see vv. 15–16).

Then David spoke to the Lord when he saw the angel who was striking down the people, and said,

113

> "Behold, it is I who have sinned, and it is I who
> have done wrong; but these sheep, what have they
> done? Please let Thy hand be against me and against
> my father's house." (v. 17)

His pride completely forsaken, David pleads with the Lord to spare the people and, in so doing, reveals a *mature attitude*. First, he displays an attitude of integrity. "I'm to blame," he admits. Second, an attitude of humility: "Let Thy hand be against me."

Then the prophet Gad arrives and instructs David to build "an altar to the Lord on the threshing floor of Araunah the Jebusite" (v. 18b). Determined to prove his sincerity, the king responds with a third attitude, instant obedience:

> David went up according to the word of Gad, just
> as the Lord had commanded. (v. 19)

Araunah sees him coming and immediately bows low before him. The king offers to buy the threshing floor from him so he can build the altar (vv. 20–21). But, graciously, Araunah tells the king that he may have everything he wants—for free (vv. 22–23).

Rather than take something for nothing, however, David insists on buying the land, displaying a fourth attitude, responsible stewardship.

> However, the king said to Araunah, "No, but I will
> surely buy it from you for a price, for I will not offer
> burnt offerings to the Lord my God which cost me
> nothing." So David bought the threshing floor and
> the oxen for fifty shekels of silver. (v. 24)

David beautifully models the right way to show our devotion to the Lord: through personal sacrifice. If our service to God costs us nothing, it's not really a sacrifice. And we tend to become irresponsible and blasé about it, don't we? But when we truly give of ourselves—our money or time or emotions—our ministry means everything to us. The Lord feels the love we invest in it, and He is pleased.

A Mature Spirit

The final scene of this story illustrates a *spirit of complete obedience*. It pictures the king in his royal splendor, sacrificing his pride on the altar of confession. No longer the all-powerful monarch, David is just a softened man talking and weeping with his God. It's a tender moment, almost too sacred to watch.

> And David built there an altar to the Lord, and offered burnt offerings and peace offerings. Thus the Lord was moved by entreaty for the land, and the plague was held back from Israel. (v. 25)

A Message: The Lessons for Adults Today

The story is over, but the truths linger on. Paul said we'd profit from our journey through the Old Testament world. Remember the three qualities he said we'd learn? First, we learn a lesson about perseverance: *When we fail . . . we do not quit.* Adult Christians are able to face the truth about themselves; they admit their sin rather than blame others, accept the consequences, and move on.

Second, we learn about encouragement: *When we obey . . . we do not argue.* It takes courage to not only admit wrong and ask forgiveness but also to humbly do the right thing without fighting back.

And finally, we learn about hope: *When we sacrifice . . . we do not lose.* The world would be puzzled by David meekly obeying the Lord. "Get off your knees and tell God He's being unfair," some people might shout. But David saw things differently. By losing himself to God, he gained life. In sacrificing his pride, he found peace.

Living Insights

When David was young, he slew the mighty Goliath with a single stone. And the women danced and sang his praises:

> "Saul has slain his thousands,
> And David his ten thousands." (1 Sam. 18:7)

But his greatest fight was yet to come. This contest didn't rage in a valley, surrounded by armies. His soul was the battleground for this fight, and nobody was there to witness it. For when he was old and alone, he battled his own pride . . . and won.

Most people would rather face a spear-throwing Goliath than cross swords with their own pride. Do you feel prepared to enter the battlefield of your soul? Take a moment to ask for the Lord's strength. And invite Him to help search out your enemy (see Ps. 139:23–24).

Pride can be cunning. Perhaps some of the following personalized statements of confession will uncover its hiding place in your heart.

- I wanted my way, regardless of what God said.
- Rather than depend on God, I gloried in my own strengths—my material wealth, my education, my successes in life.
- I refused to listen to counsel.
- I blamed others when I got caught doing something wrong.
- I gave excuses for my mistakes rather than admitting them.
- Although I said I was wrong, I still felt justified in my behavior.
- I refused to accept the consequences for my bad choices.
- I refused to admit that others were hurt because of my mistake.
- I argued that the law was unfair rather than admit failure.
- I grudgingly obeyed the Lord with the least amount of effort.

Do you see the prophet Gad's finger pointing at you through any of these statements? Which ones? What was the situation? Use the following space to contend with your pride before the Lord.

_____

_____

_____

_____

_____

Lay your pride on the altar, and as the smoke rises toward heaven, receive God's forgiveness through Christ.

> For He delivered us from the domain of darkness, and transferred us to the kingdom of His beloved Son, in whom we have redemption, the forgiveness of sins. (Col. 1:13–14)

Now respond with humble obedience. Is the Lord telling you to repair any damages your pride may have caused?

In a strange sort of way, isn't it comforting to know that David wasn't perfect? We're not glad that he messed up, of course, but it does reassure us that we all make mistakes from time to time, no matter how old we are. Do you ever feel the pressure to be perfect? Are you putting the squeeze on yourself, perhaps? How?

_____

_____

_____

That pressure can hamper your ability to constructively deal with your mistakes. Even though David made a tragic blunder, he didn't compound it by rationalizing it or hiding from it. Let's review the maturity he displayed after he sinned:

He listened to his conscience and owned up to his sin.

He relied on his theology to help him make the difficult decisions that followed.

His attitude reflected integrity, humility, willingness to obey, and responsibility.

His spirit was submissive to the Lord's will.

Perhaps you've recently made a wrong choice, but for fear of being found out, you've been covering it up. In what ways can you follow David's example and handle it with maturity?

_____

_____

_____

Chapter 15

A SONG FOR ADULTS TO SING
Psalm 26

As we grow through life with God, we often need inspiration to spur us on as well as refreshment to give us rest. The Lord's gift of music can provide both for us. Martin Luther, who you may be surprised to know wrote the hymn "A Mighty Fortress Is Our God," affirmed the spiritual role of music:

> Next to the preaching of the Scriptures, I afford music the highest place in the church. I want the Word of God to dwell in the hearts of believers by means of songs.
>
> There is a root-like unity of music and theology. Music is wrapped and locked in theology.
>
> I would allow no man to preach or teach God's people who did not realize the power and use of sacred music.[1]

So vital is music to our growth that God set aside the largest book in the Bible as a collection of songs—the Psalms. For centuries, the Psalter has been known as "The Hymnbook of the Hebrews." No book of popular ditties or shallow lyrics, it contains a vast ocean of theological wealth, the depths of which beckon us to come and explore.

Music for the Mature: A Brief Overview

Upon first entering the psalmist's world, we might feel like awkward strangers. Indeed, the rhythms and patterns of his poetry are unfamiliar. But in no time, the themes and feelings he expresses meld our hearts with his. Theologian G. Campbell Morgan commented on the remarkable way the psalms mirror our emotions.

1. Martin Luther, as quoted by Kenneth W. Osbeck in *The Endless Song* (Grand Rapids, Mich.: Kregel Publications, 1987), p. 71.

Whatever your mood, and I suppose you have changing moods as well as I do, if you could tell me sincerely and accurately, I can find you a Psalm that
will help to express it. Are you glad? I can find you
a Psalm that you can sing. Are you sad? I can find
you a Psalm that will suit that occasion. . . . The
Psalms range over the whole gamut of human
emotions. . . . But now hear me carefully. They
were all written for us in the consciousness of and
in the sense of the presence of God. . . . That gives
peculiar character to the Book of Psalms.[2]

This book of spiritual songs gives us permission to weep, to
dance, to shake our fists in anger. But never does it let us shift our
focus from God. In this way, poetry and theology are united in
perfect harmony.

One psalm that beautifully illustrates this union is Psalm 26.
This ancient song speaks particularly to those of us on the road to
spiritual adulthood who long for God to guide our emotions—
specifically, the emotions that erupt when we are wronged.

Song for the Spiritually Minded: A Careful Analysis

All of us have been taken advantage of at some time in our
lives. Call it what you will, we've all been used, manipulated, ripped
off, and betrayed. When that happens, a whole caldron of emotions
boils to the surface, ranging from confusion to anger to resentment
to revenge. If we're not careful, these feelings can easily spill over
into destructive, childish actions. Through the lyrics of this song,
David shows us the right thing to do when we've been wronged.

Although we don't know the particulars, David has been on
the receiving end of a battering ram of mistreatment. The first words
out of his mouth are:

Vindicate me, O Lord. (Ps. 26:1a)

Webster's defines *vindicate* broadly, using the synonyms "defend,"
"avenge," and "justify."[3] In Hebrew, the word depicts a courtroom

---

2. G. Campbell Morgan, *The Unfolding Message of the Bible* (Westwood, N.J.: Fleming H.
Revell Co., 1961), pp. 232–33.

3. *Merriam-Webster's Collegiate Dictionary*, 10th ed., see "vindicate."

scene where the falsely accused David pleads with God to vindicate him—to "execute judgment."[4] God alone knows the true facts, and only He is qualified to judge accurately and without prejudice.

David feels confident the verdict will come out in his favor for two reasons:

> For I have walked in my integrity;
> And I have trusted in the Lord without wavering.
> (v. 1b)

Instead of greasing palms or hiring slick lawyers, David defends himself by calling upon the silent attributes of his character. First on the witness stand is his integrity, and next, his unwavering trust in God. He is clean before the world, and before the Lord, he's secure.

In Hebrew, the word translated "wavering" is *maad*, which means "slip, slide, totter, shake."[5] David is saying, "I have trusted in the Lord, and I will not slip back and trust in my own strength. Any defending to be done the Lord will handle." David plans to keep his eyes on the Lord and continue living the way he always has—in integrity (see v. 11a).

But what about David's churning emotions? What can he do to keep his mind on the Lord and his actions pure? Verses 2–12 describe the steps he takes—steps maturing Christians will want to follow.

Be Open before the Lord

When someone takes a swipe at us, our first response is usually to swipe back. David, however, unclenches his fists and opens his hands toward heaven.

> Examine me, O Lord, and try me;
> Test my mind and my heart. (v. 2)

Before he does anything, David invites the Lord's scrutiny— not of the situation but of himself. He draws back the curtain around his heart and bids God to come and probe his inner being. Let's take a close look at how he does this by noting the three verbs he chooses.

---

4. William Gesenius, *A Hebrew and English Lexicon of the Old Testament*, trans. Edward Robinson, ed. Francis Brown, S. R. Driver, Charles A. Briggs (Oxford, England: Clarendon Press, n.d.), p. 1047.

5. Gesenius, *Hebrew and English Lexicon*, p. 588.

1. *Examine me.* David wants the Lord to search his motives and thoughts and bring to light his integrity as well as any hidden sin (see Ps. 139:23–24).

2. *Try me.* He asks God to intensify the test to humble him and prove his true character (see Deut. 8:2).

3. *Test me.* He wants God to refine his mind and heart, as a smelter refines silver, to melt away the dross and purify the precious qualities (see Zech. 13:8–9).

When you are wronged, try to remember David's prayer. Be open to what the Lord may be teaching you through this trial (see James 1:2–4).

Remembering God's Love, Continue to Obey

Throughout the ordeal, also remember God's love. The tempter will sow seeds of doubt in your mind: *How could God let this happen? Does He really love me?* These seeds tend to sprout into shoots of cynicism, then little saplings of disobedience, and eventually, a giant redwood of rebellion. David says, "That won't happen to me!"

> For Thy lovingkindness is before my eyes,
> And I have walked in Thy truth. (Ps. 26:3)

Refuse to Spend Time with Wrong Associates

We must warn you, now, some people will try to pull you off the path of obedience. David lists four types with whom he refuses to keep company for that very reason:

> I do not sit with deceitful men,
> Nor will I go with pretenders.
> I hate the assembly of evildoers,
> And I will not sit with the wicked. (vv. 4–5)

Sometimes even friends will steer you in the wrong direction when you come to them for advice. With good intentions, they'll take up the sword on your behalf and counsel you to fight back. A friend of David's once gave him this kind of advice.

Late one night, David and Abishai made an unannounced visit to King Saul, who had been spearheading a manhunt to kill David. As the two men tiptoed into camp, they spied the sleeping king. Next to his royal head was his spear, stuck in the ground (see 1 Sam. 26:6–7). The loyal Abishai suggested to David,

> "Today God has delivered your enemy into your

hand; now therefore, please let me strike him with the spear to the ground with one stroke, and I will not strike him the second time." (v. 8)

David, however, stood firm:

"Do not destroy him, for who can stretch out his hand against the Lord's anointed and be without guilt?" David also said, "As the Lord lives, surely the Lord will strike him, or his day will come that he dies, or he will go down into battle and perish." (vv. 9–10)

Who are you listening to during your trial? Is their advice honoring to the Lord? From a human point of view, it may sound like a quick and easy solution; but is it the right thing to do?

Maintain a Positive Attitude

David not only does the right thing, he does it with the right attitude.

I shall wash my hands in innocence,
And I will go about Thine altar, O Lord,
That I may proclaim with the voice of thanksgiving,
And declare all Thy wonders. (Ps. 26:6–7)

As David worships before the laver and the altar, notice that he's positive: he's praising God and he's thankful. The natural response to mistreatment is to complain. But that only breeds the emotional cancers of resentment and bitterness. How therapeutic, though, is a heart of gratitude, for it refocuses our minds on the Lord and His healing presence.

Like David, the apostles were able to maintain a grateful attitude during persecution. The high priest ordered them flogged and warned them "to speak no more in the name of Jesus" (Acts 5:40). But rather than complaining about the unfairness of it all,

they went on their way from the presence of the Council, rejoicing that they had been considered worthy to suffer shame for His name. And every day, in the temple and from house to house, they kept right on teaching and preaching Jesus as the Christ. (vv. 41–42)

"Wait a minute," we retort. "They were apostles. For us average believers, being grateful during suffering is difficult." We may mouth the words, "Thank you, God," but on the inside, we're thinking, "Thanks a *lot*, God."

The reason this point of how to respond maturely is so important is that the longer we walk with God, the more we can expect to wrestle with Him through life's painful processes. One woman wrote insightfully,

> In the commencement of the spiritual life, our hard-est task is to bear with our neighbor; in its progress, with ourselves; and in its end, with God.[6]

In those times when we least understand God, it will be a struggle to stay close to Him. Only a mature heart and mind will keep us where we need to be.

Be Faithful in Public Worship

One way David stayed close to God was through the community of worship.

> O Lord, I love the habitation of Thy house,
> And the place where Thy glory dwells.
> Do not take my soul away along with sinners,
> Nor my life with men of bloodshed. (Ps. 26:8–9)

No wonder God considered David "a man after My heart" (Acts 13:22b). Although struggling and bruised, he consistently flew like a wounded bird to the hand of his divine Master. Sometimes when our souls are bleeding, we long to flee from God and isolate ourselves from other Christians. But, according to Hebrews 10:24–25, running away is not the answer. Instead, we're urged to

> consider how to stimulate one another to love and good deeds, not forsaking our own assembling together, as is the habit of some, but encouraging one another; and all the more, as you see the day drawing near.

Patiently Stand and Wait for Relief

When help seems slow in coming, we're tempted to take matters

---

6. Attributed to Madame Guyon. Jeanne-Marie de la Motte Guyon was a "central figure in the theological debates of 17th-century France." *Encyclopaedia Britannica*, 15th ed., see "Guyon, Jeanne-Marie de la Motte."

into our own hands. But David's example reminds us to stand firm.

> But as for me, I shall walk in my integrity;
> Redeem me, and be gracious to me.
> My *foot stands on a level place;*
> In the congregations I shall bless the Lord.
> (Ps. 26:11–12, emphasis added)

Time and again, David must have been tempted to throw off his gloves and fight dirty—eye for eye and tooth for tooth. But his stance of faith was steady. In Hebrew, the word *mishor* refers to an "elevated plateau or table-land."[7] David patiently waited for God on a plateau of wisdom that provided him a panoramic view of the issues. A vengeful, tit-for-tat response would have clouded his perspective; but by waiting, he could deal with his mistreatment from God's vantage point.

Truth for Today: A Practical Response

Comprising a fitting refrain to David's song to adult Christians are Peter's thoughts in 1 Peter 2:18–20.

> Servants, be submissive to your masters with all respect, not only to those who are good and gentle, but also to those who are unreasonable. For this finds favor, if for the sake of conscience toward God a man bears up under sorrows when suffering unjustly. For what credit is there if, when you sin and are harshly treated, you endure it with patience? But if when you do what is right and suffer for it you patiently endure it, this finds favor with God.

These verses show us that, first, *mature believers want to please God, regardless.* Like David, they focus on finding favor with God, not people. Second, *they model the life of Christ.* Displaying Jesus' qualities while suffering is more important to them than coming out on top. Third, *they see benefit in hardship.* Through the pain, they cling even more to the Savior's side. And for that reason alone, it's worth it all.

---

7. Gesenius, *Hebrew and English Lexicon*, p. 449.

No one has to teach a child the definition of the word *fair*. In a child's mind, *fair* means, "If I have to pick up my toys, my sister has to pick up hers too." Or, "If my brother gets a piece of pie, I get exactly the same-sized piece . . . to the crumb." *Fair* means good guys always win and bad guys always lose. Fairness is the emotional gravity in a child's world that makes life predictable and safe.

But somewhere between childhood and adulthood, everything turns upside down. In real life, good guys often lose and bad guys get off the hook. Bosses renege on their promises. Former friends spread lies about us. And people who borrow money refuse to repay. As people take advantage of us, we want to stamp our feet and shout, "That's not fair!" But we're afraid that won't do any good. We feel like we're floating in a world without the gravity of justice, and we yearn to hold on to something solid.

Has someone treated you unfairly lately? It may be a small matter, but it's enough to make you feel disillusioned with people and the unjust world we live in. What is the situation?

_____

_____

What was your initial emotional response to this mistreatment?

_____

_____

Review the six steps David recommended:

- Be open before the Lord.

- Remembering God's love, continue to obey Him.

- Refuse to spend time with wrong associates.

- Maintain a positive attitude.

- Be faithful in public worship.

- Patiently stand and wait for relief.

What are some ways you can follow these steps? You may want

to begin opening yourself to the Lord by sincerely praying David's prayer in Psalm 26:2–3. Then, in the following space, jot down your plans to accomplish the rest of the steps.

_____

_____

_____

_____

Remember, there *is* something to hold on to in our topsy-turvy world—or, according to David, some One to hold on to.

> And he said,
> "The Lord is my rock and my fortress and my
>   deliverer;
> My God, my rock, in whom I take refuge;
> My shield and the horn of my salvation, my
>   stronghold and my refuge;
> My savior, Thou dost save me from violence."
> (2 Sam. 22:2–3)

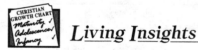

Living Insights

Henry Gariepy describes the precious insights trials provide us:

> The Arabs have a proverb: "All sunshine makes a desert." (They ought to know.) When life is easy, it is possible to live on the surface of things. But when trial and sorrow come, then one is driven to the deeper things. Then one can enter into the secrets and beauties of God. It is in the storm that God arches His rainbow over us, its multi-splendor revealing all the elements of color that make up the beauty of the world. Life's greatest revelations come in its storms.[8]

8. Henry Gariepy, *Portraits of Perseverance* (Wheaton, Ill.: Scripture Press Publications, Victor Books, 1989), pp. 127–28.

Like a six-year-old watching a monster movie, though, we tend to bury our eyes in our hands when an ugly trial jumps into the scene. As a result, we miss the best parts of life's unfolding drama!

If you're enduring a hard time, you may not be able to see any good coming out of it because it's all too scary right now. But when the lights come on and the credits roll, you'll probably have a better perspective of "the deeper things" Gariepy is talking about. Until then, peek through your fingers and look intently at your trial. Then take a few moments to be quiet and listen to the Lord's still voice.

What rainbow revelations is He arching over your life? Your priorities? Your goals? Your relationships? Take a few moments to think this over. We'll provide you some space to write down what you discover.[9]

———————————————————————————

———————————————————————————

———————————————————————————

———————————————————————————

———————————————————————————

9. Adapted from the study guide *What It Takes to Win*, coauthored by Bryce Klabunde, from the Bible-teaching ministry of Charles R. Swindoll (Anaheim, Calif.: Insight for Living, 1993), pp. 94–95.

Chapter 16

GROWING-UP GOALS FOR DILIGENT DISCIPLES

2 Peter 1:1–11

Back in 1972, a number of eagles in Idaho, Nevada, and Oregon were dying in an unusual way. They were being electrocuted while nesting among power lines. For the Idaho Power Company, writes journalist Michael Rozek,

> this was the worst kind of publicity, especially when pictures of the eagles appeared in local newspapers: the birds were noble and beautiful, an endangered species protected by federal law, and they were being killed, it seemed, by brute technology.[1]

Ever since the days of Thomas Edison, birds had perched atop power lines. Why were these eagles suddenly getting electrocuted from them? The company hired naturalist and falconer Morlan Nelson to find out. With some mock cables set up in his backyard, he observed his own eagles landing on them.

> He realized that when the birds perched, because of their six- to seven-foot wingspan, they routinely touched two line conductors, or a conductor and a ground wire, at once, electrocuting them[selves].[2]

Having solved the mystery, Nelson advised the company to construct safe perches for the eagles on top of the poles so their wings wouldn't touch two lines at the same time. And it worked!

Like those eagles, we can also be endangered by "power lines." How? Enthusiastic about the Christian life, we can touch one "wing" to the power line of *idealism*, while another unavoidably brushes against the ground wire of *reality*. Suddenly, without warning, we get zapped with disillusionment and our faith comes crashing to the ground.

The best protection against such a shock is to balance our

1. Michael Rozek, "Friend and Protector," *Western's World*, May 1985, p. 32.
2. Rozek, "Friend and Protector," p. 32.

Christian ideals with a realistic understanding of spiritual growth. So let's take a moment to review what we've learned about the growth process so far.

A Review of the Ages and Stages

First, everyone becomes a member of God's family through new *birth*. Then we enter *infancy*, in which we are eager yet fragile in our faith and must depend on others to feed us the milk of God's Word. Next comes *childhood*. This is a time for exciting discoveries as we learn to feed ourselves and walk on our own. *Adolescence* is a period when we challenge the truths we've always been taught and strive to define our own identity as Christians. The last stage is *adulthood*, but even in this stage we don't stop growing. The apostle Paul acknowledged:

> I haven't learned all I should even yet, but I keep working toward that day when I will finally be all that Christ saved me for and wants me to be.
> No, dear brothers, I am still not all I should be but I am bringing all my energies to bear on this one thing: Forgetting the past and looking forward to what lies ahead, I strain to reach the end of the race and receive the prize for which God is calling us up to heaven because of what Christ Jesus did for us. (Phil. 3:12b–14 LB)

Even Paul never reached a plateau of complete maturity. So, you see, it's idealistic to think we can skip stages or know God's truth so well that we have an answer for every problem. We're mistaken if we assume that we've "arrived" spiritually and will no longer struggle with sin. The reality is that we must continually "bring all our energies" to getting up the hill toward Christlikeness. As adult Christians, we must expect to sometimes slip back into adolescence or childhood, but that's not the end of the world. "Forgetting the past," we accept God's forgiveness for our mistakes and keep going.

One of the most idealistic disciples was Peter. Full of bravado, he announced to Christ, "Even if I have to die with You, I will not deny You" (Matt. 26:35). But soon after, he came in contact with the ground wire of reality and denied the Lord three times (vv. 69–75). The devastating disillusionment might have killed his faith had not

Jesus lovingly restored him after the Resurrection (see John 21:1–19).

Peter certainly understood the difficulties of growing up in God's family. And he, more than anyone, can help prepare us for what's ahead.

A Plea for Balance and Obedience

Despite his discouraging experience, Peter doesn't recommend that we toss out all our Christian ideals. Far from that, he advises us simply to keep them in balance with the more down-to-earth aspects of our faith. For example, he begins his second epistle by painting a glorious portrait of the child of God, dressed in the sumptuous robes of God's blessings.

> Grace and peace be multiplied to you in the knowledge of God and of Jesus our Lord; seeing that His divine power has granted to us everything pertaining to life and godliness, through the true knowledge of Him who called us by His own glory and excellence. For by these He has granted to us His precious and magnificent promises, in order that by them you might become partakers of the divine nature, having escaped the corruption that is in the world by lust. (2 Pet. 1:2–4)

Through Christ, God has decked us out with limitless power for growth. He has draped us in His "precious and magnificent promises" of strength, rewards, and comfort. And by virtue of our spiritual birthright, we carry His very nature within us—a nature that will enable us to escape the corruption of a world driven by lust.

Amazing! We have everything we need to live godly lives. Theologians call our spiritual resources "divine enablement." But Peter doesn't put his pen down yet. Balancing this doctrine with everyday human responsibility, he goes on to explain what we must supply to achieve the goal of a godly life.

> Now for this very reason also, applying all *diligence*
> . . . (v. 5a, emphasis added)

God provides the power and the promises; we supply the diligence. The Greek term means "to make haste, be eager . . . to do one's best, to take care, to exert one's self."[3] Diligence serves as a

3. Kenneth S. Wuest, *In These Last Days* (Grand Rapids, Mich.: William B. Eerdmans Publishing Co., 1954), p. 22.

130

catalyst that releases God's power and brings about change. It transforms theory into reality.

Are we left to our imaginations to figure out how to accomplish this? Not at all. Through Peter, God spells out several crucial goals and objectives that are worth our diligent effort.

A List of Goals and Objectives

Our goals, or the expectations of spiritual adulthood, can be boiled down to eight essentials.

Expectations

Now for this very reason also, applying all diligence, in your faith supply moral excellence, and in your moral excellence, knowledge; and in your knowledge, self-control, and in your self-control, perseverance, and in your perseverance, godliness; and in your godliness, brotherly kindness, and in your brotherly kindness, love. (vv. 5–7)

Let's take a moment to carefully examine each trait listed in this passage.[4]

Faith. Faith is the foundation of the Christian life; it's the firm conviction that God's Word is true. In practical terms, it means confidently abandoning ourselves to His will, His strength, and His wisdom.

Peter says, "In your faith *supply.* . . ." Let's zero in on that word for a moment. The Greek term is *epichorēgeō*, which—as is implicit in its English derivative, *chorus*—has to do with the theater. Originally, the word referred to a wealthy benefactor who "supplied" or financed lavish Greek plays. Later, the definition broadened, meaning,

to supply in copious measure, to provide beyond the need, to supply more than generously.[5]

Peter doesn't want us just to believe in God; he wants us to richly add to our beliefs the following seven qualities.

Moral excellence. Excellence in anything is measured against its

---

4. The following section has been adapted from "To Be Useful and Fruitful, Here's How," from the study guide *Conquering through Conflict: A Study of 2 Peter*, coauthored by Lee Hough, from the Bible-teaching ministry of Charles R. Swindoll (Fullerton, Calif.: Insight for Living, 1990), pp. 14–15.

5. Wuest, *In These Last Days*, p. 23.

intended purpose. A knife is excellent if it cuts well; a field, if it produces a bumper harvest. Our standard of excellence is Jesus Christ. The more we resemble Him in our actions and attitudes, the more we become the kind of people God created us to be.

Knowledge. This isn't theoretical knowledge. The Greek term, *gnōsis,* refers to practical knowledge, a commonsense approach to applying biblical principles in our daily circumstances.

Self-control. Literally, this word means "the ability to take a grip of oneself."[6] Nothing is to master us but the Master Himself—not work, sex, food, or any of those things that can so easily take over our lives. Self-control means that, with God's help, we can live a more balanced life—even in a world where overindulgence is hyped as the highway to happiness.

Perseverance. In Greek, this word literally means "to remain under." Even though the load of difficulties and distresses in our lives weighs heavily on our shoulders, we stand our ground. Perseverance takes courage to accept what life throws at us and to hold on to our beliefs and standards, regardless.

Godliness. This refers to a two-sided authentic piety. First, there's a right attitude toward God, reflected in worship and obedience. Second, there's a right attitude toward others, evidenced by respectfulness and a servant's heart.

Brotherly kindness. The brotherly kindness, *philadelphia,* that Christ intends for us to display involves bearing one another's burdens (see Gal. 6:2). We're to come out of our theological ivory towers and get involved in helping others in the trenches of life. We need to make room for other people's opinions, feelings, and suggestions. And we've got to be willing to see life through their eyes.

Christian love. The top rung of Peter's eight-step ladder is love. It's the one virtue that comprises and unites all the others. Using the letters in the word, we can identify its components:

L— *Listen.* I listen intently to other people's words and feelings.

O— *Overlook.* I overlook other people's minor differences and petty faults.

V— *Value.* I value the people I love, treating them with dignity.

E— *Express.* I express my feelings by giving of myself.[7]

6. William Barclay, *The Letters of James and Peter,* rev. ed., The Daily Study Bible Series (Philadelphia, Pa.: Westminster Press, 1976), p. 302.

7. The acrostic is adapted from *Seeds of Greatness,* by Denis Waitley (Old Tappan, N.J.: Fleming H. Revell Co., 1983), p. 134.

What a list! It's no wonder Peter prefaces it with the assurance of divine power and the need for diligence. In the next verses, he exhorts us to cultivate these qualities in our lives, describing the positive consequences if we do, and the negative if we don't.

Exhortations

> For if these qualities are yours and are increasing, they render you neither useless nor unfruitful in the true knowledge of our Lord Jesus Christ. For he who lacks these qualities is blind or shortsighted, having forgotten his purification from his former sins. (2 Pet. 1:8–9)

By living out these qualities, we reach the summit of our spiritual maturity: we become useful instruments in the Master's hand and fruitful vines that nourish others and glorify the Lord. Conversely, if we neglect these characteristics, we lose sight of our goal and wander in the darkness. According to commentator Michael Green,

> Such a man is blind because he blinks or wilfully closes his eyes to the light. Spiritual blindness descends upon the eyes which deliberately look away from the graces of character to which the Christian is called when he comes to know Christ.[8]

But to those of us who yearn to grow, Peter concludes on an upbeat note with an encouraging promise:

> Therefore, brethren, be all the more diligent to make certain about His calling and choosing you; for as long as you practice these things, you will never stumble; for in this way the entrance into the eternal kingdom of our Lord and Savior Jesus Christ will be abundantly supplied to you. (vv. 10–11)

As long as we keep these things in balance—the ideal of who we are in Christ and the reality of what it takes to grow—we will walk straight and not stumble. We won't be shocked when trouble

---

8. Michael Green, *The Second Epistle General of Peter and the General Epistle of Jude* (Grand Rapids, Mich.: William B. Eerdmans Publishing Co., 1968), p. 73. The Greek term for short-sighted is *myopazon*, from which we get the English word *myopia*. *Webster's* defines *myopia* as "a lack of foresight or discernment." *Merriam-Webster's Collegiate Dictionary*, 10th ed., see "myopia."

comes because we will have within us the maturity to deal with it and keep soaring as eagles.

A Suggestion to Remember and Apply

As a final send-off, we offer this suggestion: Always remember who you are in Christ. Of course, ready yourself for the reality of living in a sinful world. But in your preparations, don't lose sight of your identity.

In Indian folklore, there's a story about a brave who placed an eagle's egg in the nest of a prairie chicken. The eaglet hatched and grew up, scratching for insects and flapping his golden wings like a common prairie chicken. One day he spied a magnificent bird flying above him and gazed longingly as it soared effortlessly among the clouds. One of the prairie chickens clucked at him, "That's an eagle—the chief of the birds. But don't give it a second thought. You could never be like him." And the eaglet never did think of it again, living out his days earthbound as the prairie chickens around him.[9]

Soaring in the lofty heights of spiritual maturity may seem like a distant dream right now. But it's not an impossible dream. You have what it takes, because "His divine power has granted to us everything pertaining to life and godliness" (2 Pet. 1:3a). You're an eagle! Test the wings God gave you by putting into practice some of the qualities from this chapter.

And fly!

 Living Insights STUDY ONE

Would you like to start testing your wings right now? Let's begin with a short flight for practice. Pick one of the qualities of maturity from the following list and jot down how you could put it into action this week.

Faith	Perseverance
Moral Excellence	Godliness
Knowledge	Brotherly Kindness

9. Adapted from a story by Ted W. Engstrom in _The Pursuit of Excellence_ (Grand Rapids, Mich.: Zondervan Publishing House, 1982), pp. 15–16.

_____

_____

_____

_____

As you gain strength and confidence, try for a longer flight by living out this quality, for say, two weeks or a month. Tell someone that you are trying to grow in that area so they can encourage you. Then pick another one and put wings on it. In no time, you'll be soaring.

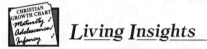 **_Living Insights_**   STUDY TWO

In this chapter, we said that the best protection against crashing is to balance our Christian ideals with a realistic understanding of spiritual growth. Thinking back over the entire guide, how has our study helped you gain a better understanding of growing up in God's family? You may wish to thumb through the study guide to pull out some of the principles that meant the most to you.

_____

_____

_____

_____

In chapter 4, we asked you to pinpoint which stage of growth you thought best described you. Having completed the study, do you still think you're in that stage? Do some of the characteristics of the other stages describe you at times as well? Place an X where you fit on the snail's shell now.

Sometimes it may seem like you're growing at a snail's pace, but at other times, as fast as a rabbit. What factors tend to hinder your spiritual growth, and what factors help it?

_____

_____

_____

_____

_____

According to Peter, God has "called us by His own glory and excellence" (2 Pet. 1:3b). And if He has called us as His own, He knows us and has designed a plan of growth for us that stretches far beyond today. In the weeks ahead, what will it take for you to follow that plan for your life?

_____

_____

_____

_____

In conclusion, we leave you with this prayer. Apply it daily to your heart. Let it express your desire to press on to maturity and become the person God wants you to be.

> Almighty God, you who have made all things for me, and me for your glory, sanctify my body and soul, my thoughts and my intentions, my words and actions, that whatsoever I shall think, or speak, or do, may by me be designed to the glorification of your name. And let no pride or self-seeking, no impure motive or unworthy purpose, no little ends or low imagination stain my spirit, or profane any of my words and actions. But let my body be a servant to my spirit, and both body and spirit servants of Jesus Christ.[10]

10. Thomas À Kempis, as quoted in The One Year Book of Personal Prayer (Wheaton, Ill.: Tyndale House Publishers, 1991), p. 260.

BOOKS FOR
PROBING FURTHER

A good book always makes for a welcome traveling companion. We've compiled a few of our favorites that you may wish to take with you on your journey of spiritual growth.

Anders, Max E. *30 Days to Understanding the Christian Life*. Brentwood, Tenn.: Wolgemuth and Hyatt, Publishers, 1990.

Hendricks, Howard G., and William D. Hendricks. *Living by the Book*. Chicago, Ill.: Moody Press, 1991.

Peterson, Eugene H. *A Long Obedience in the Same Direction*. Downers Grove, Ill.: InterVarsity Press, 1980.

Sanders, J. Oswald. *In Pursuit of Maturity*. Grand Rapids, Mich.: Zondervan Publishing House, Lamplighter Books, 1986.

Strauss, Richard L. *Growing More like Jesus*. Neptune, N.J.: Loizeaux Brothers, 1991.

White, John. *Magnificent Obsession*. Revised edition. Downers Grove, Ill.: InterVarsity Press, 1990.

Whitney, Donald S. *Spiritual Disciplines for the Christian Life*. Colorado Springs, Colo.: NavPress, 1991.

Some of the books listed above may be out of print and available only through a library. For those currently available, please contact your local Christian bookstore. Books by Charles R. Swindoll are available through Insight for Living. IFL also offers some books by other authors—please note the ordering information that follows and contact the office that serves you.

ORDERING INFORMATION

GROWING UP IN GOD'S FAMILY

Cassette Tapes and Study Guide

This Bible study guide was designed to be used independently or in conjunction with the broadcast of Chuck Swindoll's taped messages which are listed below. If you would like to order cassette tapes or further copies of this study guide, please see the information given below and the order forms provided at the end of this guide.

		U.S.	Canada
GUF SG	Study guide	$ 4.95	$ 6.50
GUF CS	Cassette series,	55.15	65.75
	includes album cover		
GUF 1–8	Individual cassettes,	ea. 6.30	ea. 8.50
	includes messages A and B		

The prices are subject to change without notice.

GUF 1-A: *Analysis of a Crop Failure*—Mark 4:1–20
      B: *Growing Up in God's Family*—Selected Scriptures

GUF 2-A: *Ages and Stages of Growing Up*—Selected Scriptures
      B: *Birth and Infancy: Survival Basics*—Selected Scriptures

GUF 3-A: *Look . . . I'm Walking!*—Ephesians 5:1–8, 15–21
      B: *The Delights of Childhood*—Selected Scriptures

GUF 4-A: *Adult Talk about "Childish Things"*—Selected Scriptures
      B: *Three Proofs of Growth*—Matthew 10:1–10; Acts 4:32–37

GUF 5-A: *Adolescents in Adult Bodies*—Selected Scriptures
      B: *When Peter Pan Comes to Church*—1 Corinthians 1:4–11; 3:1–4; 5:1–2; 8:1–13

GUF 6-A: *What's Right about Adolescence?*—Selected Scriptures
      B: *Reasons We Resist Becoming Mature*—Hebrews 2:1–3; 3:12–13; 4:1–2; 5:11–14

GUF 7-A: *The Church: Who Needs It?*—Selected Scriptures
      B: *A Story for Adults to Remember*—2 Samuel 24:10–25

GUF 8-A: *A Song for Adults to Sing*—Psalm 26
     B: *Growing-Up Goals for Diligent Disciples*—2 Peter 1:1–11

How to Order by Phone or FAX
(Credit card orders only)

United States: 1-800-772-8888 from 7:00 A.M. to 4:30 P.M., Pacific time, Monday through Friday
FAX (714) 575-5496 anytime, day or night

Canada: 1-800-663-7639, Vancouver residents call (604) 596-2910 from 7:00 A.M. to 5:00 P.M., Pacific time, Monday through Friday
FAX (604) 596-2975 anytime, day or night

Australia: (03) 872-4606 or FAX (03) 874-8890 from 9:00 A.M. to 5:00 P.M., Monday through Friday

---

Other International Locations: call the Ordering Services Department in the United States at (714) 575-5000 during the hours listed above.

How to Order by Mail

United States
• Mail to: Ordering Services Department
          Insight for Living
          Post Office Box 69000
          Anaheim, CA 92817-0900
• Sales tax: California residents add 7.25%.
• Shipping: add 10% of the total order amount for first-class delivery. (Otherwise, allow four to six weeks for fourth-class delivery.)
• Payment: personal checks, money orders, credit cards (Visa, MasterCard, Discover Card, and American Express). No invoices or COD orders available.
• $10 fee for *any* returned check.

Canada
• Mail to: Insight for Living Ministries
          Post Office Box 2510
          Vancouver, BC V6B 3W7
• Sales tax: please add 7% GST. British Columbia residents also add 7% sales tax (on tapes or cassette series).

140

- Shipping: included in prices listed above.
- Payment: personal checks, money orders, credit cards (Visa, Master-Card). No invoices or COD orders available.
- Delivery: approximately four weeks.

Australia, New Zealand, or Papua New Guinea
- Mail to: Insight for Living, Inc.
  GPO Box 2823 EE
  Melbourne, Victoria 3001, Australia
- Shipping and delivery time: please see chart that follows.
- Payment: personal checks payable in U.S. funds, international money orders, or credit cards (Visa, MasterCard).

Other International Locations
- Mail to: Ordering Services Department
  Insight for Living
  Post Office Box 69000
  Anaheim, CA 92817-0900
- Shipping and delivery time: please see chart that follows.
- Payment: personal checks payable in U.S. funds, international money orders, or credit cards (Visa, MasterCard, and American Express).

Type of Shipping	Postage Cost	Delivery
Surface	10% of total order*	6 to 10 weeks
Airmail	25% of total order*	under 6 weeks

Use U.S. price as a base.

Our Guarantee

Your complete satisfaction is our top priority here at Insight for Living. If you're not completely satisfied with anything you order, please return it for full credit, a refund, or a replacement, as *you* prefer.

Insight for Living Catalog

The Insight for Living catalog features study guides, tapes, and books by a variety of Christian authors. To obtain a free copy, call us at the numbers listed above.

Order Form
United States, Australia, and Other International Locations
(Canadian residents please use order form on reverse side.)

GUF CS represents the entire *Growing Up in God's Family* series in a special album cover, while GUF 1–8 are the individual tapes included in the series. GUF SG represents this study guide, should you desire to order additional copies.

GUF	SG	Study guide	$ 4.95
GUF	CS	Cassette series, includes album cover	55.15
GUF	1–8	Individual cassettes, includes messages A and B	ea. 6.30

Product Code	Product Description	Quantity	Unit Price	Total
			$	$
		Subtotal		
		California Residents—Sales Tax *Add 7.25% of subtotal.*		
		U.S. First-Class Shipping *For faster delivery, add 10% for postage and handling.*		
		Non-United States Residents *U.S. price plus 10% surface postage or 25% airmail.*		
		Gift to Insight for Living *Tax-deductible in the United States.*		
		Total Amount Due *Please do not send cash.*		$

Prices are subject to change without notice.

Payment by: ❏ Check or money order payable to Insight for Living   ❏ Credit card

(Circle one):   Visa   MasterCard   Discover Card   American Express

Number＿＿＿＿＿＿＿＿＿＿＿＿＿＿＿＿＿＿＿＿＿＿＿＿＿＿＿

Expiration Date＿＿＿＿＿＿   Signature＿＿＿＿＿＿＿＿＿＿＿＿＿＿＿
We cannot process your credit card purchase without your signature.

Name＿＿＿＿＿＿＿＿＿＿＿＿＿＿＿＿＿＿＿＿＿＿＿＿＿＿＿＿＿

Address＿＿＿＿＿＿＿＿＿＿＿＿＿＿＿＿＿＿＿＿＿＿＿＿＿＿＿＿

City＿＿＿＿＿＿＿＿＿＿＿＿＿＿＿＿＿＿   State＿＿＿＿＿＿

Zip Code＿＿＿＿＿＿＿＿＿   Country＿＿＿＿＿＿＿＿＿＿＿＿

Telephone (＿＿＿)＿＿＿＿＿＿＿＿＿＿＿   Radio Station＿＿ ＿＿ ＿＿ ＿＿
If questions arise concerning your order, we may need to contact you.

Mail this order form to the Ordering Services Department at one of these addresses:

Insight for Living
Post Office Box 69000, Anaheim, CA 92817-0900

Insight for Living, Inc.
GPO Box 2823 EE, Melbourne, VIC 3001, Australia

Order Form
Canadian Residents

(Residents of the United States, Australia, and other international locations, please use order form on reverse side.)

GUF CS represents the entire *Growing Up in God's Family* series in a special album cover, while GUF 1–8 are the individual tapes included in the series. GUF SG represents this study guide, should you desire to order additional copies.

GUF	SG	Study guide	$ 6.50
GUF	CS	Cassette series, includes album cover	65.75
GUF	1–8	Individual cassettes, includes messages A and B	ea. 8.50

Product Code	Product Description	Quantity	Unit Price	Total
			$	$
		Subtotal		
		Add 7% GST		
		British Columbia Residents *Add 7% sales tax on individual tapes or cassette series.*		
		Gift to Insight for Living Ministries *Tax-deductible in Canada.*		
		Total Amount Due *Please do not send cash.*	$	

Prices are subject to change without notice.

Payment by: ❑ Check or money order payable to Insight for Living Ministries
❑ Credit card

(Circle one): Visa   MasterCard   Number _____

Expiration Date _____   Signature _____
We cannot process your credit card purchase without your signature.

Name _____

Address _____

City _____   Province _____

Postal Code _____   Country _____

Telephone (___) _____   Radio Station ____ ____ ____ ____
If questions arise concerning your order, we may need to contact you.

Mail this order form to the Ordering Services Department at the following address:

Insight for Living Ministries
Post Office Box 2510
Vancouver, BC, Canada V6B 3W7

Order Form
United States, Australia, and Other International Locations
(Canadian residents please use order form on reverse side.)

GUF CS represents the entire *Growing Up in God's Family* series in a special album cover, while GUF 1–8 are the individual tapes included in the series. GUF SG represents this study guide, should you desire to order additional copies.

GUF	SG	Study guide	$ 4.95
GUF	CS	Cassette series, includes album cover	55.15
GUF	1–8	Individual cassettes, includes messages A and B	ea. 6.30

Product Code	Product Description	Quantity	Unit Price	Total
			$	$
		Subtotal		
		California Residents—Sales Tax *Add 7.25% of subtotal.*		
		U.S. First-Class Shipping *For faster delivery, add 10% for postage and handling.*		
		Non-United States Residents *U.S. price plus 10% surface postage or 25% airmail.*		
		Gift to Insight for Living *Tax-deductible in the United States.*		
		Total Amount Due *Please do not send cash.*	$	

Prices are subject to change without notice.

Payment by: ❑ Check or money order payable to Insight for Living ❑ Credit card

(Circle one): Visa   MasterCard   Discover Card   American Express

Number _____

Expiration Date _____ Signature _____
We cannot process your credit card purchase without your signature.

Name _____

Address _____

City _____ State _____

Zip Code _____ Country _____

Telephone ( ) _____ Radio Station ____ ____ ____ ____
If questions arise concerning your order, we may need to contact you.

Mail this order form to the Ordering Services Department at one of these addresses:

Insight for Living
Post Office Box 69000, Anaheim, CA 92817-0900

Insight for Living, Inc.
GPO Box 2823 EE, Melbourne, VIC 3001, Australia

Order Form
Canadian Residents

(Residents of the United States, Australia, and other international locations,
please use order form on reverse side.)

GUF CS represents the entire *Growing Up in God's Family* series in a special album cover,
while GUF 1–8 are the individual tapes included in the series. GUF SG represents this study
guide, should you desire to order additional copies.

GUF	SG	Study guide	$ 6.50
GUF	CS	Cassette series, includes album cover	65.75
GUF	1–8	Individual cassettes, includes messages A and B	ea. 8.50

Product Code	Product Description	Quantity	Unit Price	Total
			$	$
		Subtotal		
		Add 7% GST		
		British Columbia Residents *Add 7% sales tax on individual tapes or cassette series.*		
		Gift to Insight for Living Ministries *Tax-deductible in Canada.*		
		Total Amount Due *Please do not send cash.*	$	

Prices are subject to change without notice.

Payment by: ☐ Check or money order payable to Insight for Living Ministries
☐ Credit card

(Circle one): Visa   MasterCard   Number _____

Expiration Date _____   Signature _____

We cannot process your credit card purchase without your signature.

Name _____

Address _____

City _____   Province _____

Postal Code _____   Country _____

Telephone ( ) _____   Radio Station ____ ____ ____ ____
If questions arise concerning your order, we may need to contact you.

Mail this order form to the Ordering Services Department at the following address:

Insight for Living Ministries
Post Office Box 2510
Vancouver, BC, Canada V6B 3W7

Order Form
United States, Australia, and Other International Locations
(Canadian residents please use order form on reverse side.)

GUF CS represents the entire *Growing Up in God's Family* series in a special album cover, while GUF 1–8 are the individual tapes included in the series. GUF SG represents this study guide, should you desire to order additional copies.

GUF	SG	Study guide	$ 4.95
GUF	CS	Cassette series, includes album cover	55.15
GUF	1–8	Individual cassettes, includes messages A and B	ea. 6.30

Product Code	Product Description	Quantity	Unit Price	Total
			$	$
		Subtotal		
		California Residents—Sales Tax *Add 7.25% of subtotal.*		
		U.S. First-Class Shipping *For faster delivery, add 10% for postage and handling.*		
		Non-United States Residents *U.S. price plus 10% surface postage or 25% airmail.*		
		Gift to Insight for Living *Tax-deductible in the United States.*		
		Total Amount Due *Please do not send cash.*	$	

Prices are subject to change without notice.

Payment by: ❑ Check or money order payable to Insight for Living ❑ Credit card

(Circle one): Visa   MasterCard   Discover Card   American Express

Number _____

Expiration Date _____ Signature _____

We cannot process your credit card purchase without your signature.

Name _____

Address _____

City _____ State _____

Zip Code _____ Country _____

Telephone ( ) _____ Radio Station ____ ____ ____ ____

If questions arise concerning your order, we may need to contact you.

Mail this order form to the Ordering Services Department at one of these addresses:

Insight for Living
Post Office Box 69000, Anaheim, CA 92817-0900

Insight for Living, Inc.
GPO Box 2823 EE, Melbourne, VIC 3001, Australia

ECFA MEMBER

Order Form
Canadian Residents

(Residents of the United States, Australia, and other international locations,
please use order form on reverse side.)

GUF CS represents the entire *Growing Up in God's Family* series in a special album cover,
while GUF 1–8 are the individual tapes included in the series. GUF SG represents this study
guide, should you desire to order additional copies.

GUF	SG	Study guide	$ 6.50
GUF	CS	Cassette series, includes album cover	65.75
GUF	1–8	Individual cassettes, includes messages A and B	ea. 8.50

Product Code	Product Description	Quantity	Unit Price	Total
			$	$
		Subtotal		
		Add 7% GST		
		British Columbia Residents *Add 7% sales tax on individual tapes or cassette series.*		
		Gift to Insight for Living Ministries *Tax-deductible in Canada.*		
		Total Amount Due *Please do not send cash.*	$	

Prices are subject to change without notice.

Payment by: ❑ Check or money order payable to Insight for Living Ministries
❑ Credit card

(Circle one): Visa   MasterCard   Number _____

Expiration Date _____   Signature _____
We cannot process your credit card purchase without your signature.

Name _____

Address _____

City _____   Province _____

Postal Code _____   Country _____

Telephone (____) _____   Radio Station ____ ____ ____ ____
If questions arise concerning your order, we may need to contact you.

Mail this order form to the Ordering Services Department at the following address:

Insight for Living Ministries
Post Office Box 2510
Vancouver, BC, Canada V6B 3W7